NOTES ON THE SLAVIC RELIGIO-ETHICAL LEGENDS:
THE DUALISTIC CREATION OF THE WORLD

Notes on the Slavic Religio-Ethical Legends:

The Dualistic Creation of the World

Drahomaniv

M. P. DRAGOMANOV

Translated by

EARL W. COUNT

INDIANA UNIVERSITY PUBLICATIONS
RUSSIAN AND EAST EUROPEAN SERIES, VOL. 23

Published by
INDIANA UNIVERSITY • BLOOMINGTON
Mouton & Co. • The Hague, The Netherlands
1961

RUSSIAN AND EAST EUROPEAN SERIES

RUSSIAN AND EAST EUROPEAN INSTITUTE

INDIANA UNIVERSITY

Volume 23

Composed at the

Indiana University Research Center in

Anthropology, Folklore, and Linguistics

All orders from the United States of America and from
Canada should be addressed to the
Editor, Russian and East European Series, Rayl House,
Indiana University, Bloomington, Indiana

Orders from all other countries should be sent to
Mouton & Co., Publishers, The Hague, The Netherlands

Library of Congress Catalog Card Number: 60-63854

Printed in the United States of America

TABLE OF CONTENTS

The translator is happy to acknowledge
a grant from the Wenner-Gren Foundation
for Anthropological Research which aided
him in preparing this manuscript for translation. He also wishes to thank Professor
Thomas A. Sebeok and Mr. Earl K. Brigham
for their efforts in seeing it into print.

E. W. C.

INTRODUCTION

This is a translation of an essay by the Ukrainian academician, Mixailo Petrovič Dragomanov, written originally in
Bulgarian.

There is a goodly number of reasons for rendering it into
English. No other single folk-idea is so widely held in the
world as this: that once a creator-being dived for earth to the
bottom of a primeval ocean, which material a companion creator-
being strewed upon it to make the dry land. This is the object of
Dragomanov's study.

Its roots are in the Middle East of several millennia ago,
in mankind's most fecund and dynamic culture area;* but —
unlike the records left to us from the sophisticate strata of
ancient societies, and which preoccupy the writings of history
— the tales which embody this folk-idea bespeak the mentality
of the illiterate. And let us not forget that they always were
the great bulk of ancient society.

The idea is a revealing by-product from the period which
saw the climax and death of an ancient world and the embryogenesis of another. For several decades (ending with the first
world war) there was a body of scholars, chiefly though not
exclusively Slavs, who worked over the origin and history of
the idea. In the opinion of the translator, Dragomanov's essay
ranks first among their studies.

It is an instructive example of an intellectual activity which
combines the canons of XIX century western scholarship with
a subject-matter altogether too unfamiliar to Occidental scholars, of that day as well as of this.

However, the principal reason for the translation is one
of culture-historical anthropology. Aboriginal North American
culture is reasonably presumed to contain ingredients that
passed from Eurasia eastward to this continent. If the origins
of these at all could be pinned to time and place in the Old
World, by so much the flatness of American ethnology might

---

*The force of this appraisal is hardly diminished, even if
it be insisted that the modern Occident overtops it.

be converted to the relief of history, and some of the area of
North America would become attached to the "ancient oikouméne,"
if but as a somewhat tattered fringe. And Dragomanov's study
(though that author did not favor the notion that American Indian
tales of the earth-diver had genetic connection with those of the
Old World) is, I believe, the most informative that has ever
been made of the theme, and cardinal to its study. *

II

Here we may summarize the probable historic course followed by the strange tale of the earth-diver in the primeval
ocean. It appears to stem from Sumeria — unless behind the
writings and carvings left to us from that tremendous culture
there are yet more ancient unknowns. To speak diagrammat-
ically — it represents but one line of elaboration in a web that
would finally catch up the story in Genesis on the one hand and,
possibly, the primeval sea in certain cosmogonic tales of India
and its eastward cultural outliers. Tibet and China are notably
devoid of the tale.

Mesopotamian cosmogonic notions dominated the welter of
Middle Eastern ideologies in the first millennium B.C. Screened
through Persian dualism, the complex concept escaped northward
into the Eurasiatic interior. Along various routes it took on the
guises of Manicheism, Christianity (apparently, Nestorianism
and Byzantine Orthodoxy according to circumstances), Buddhism;
even Zervanism and possibly Mazdaism. In their several ways,
Slavs, Finns, Ugrs, Turks, Mongols have fallen heirs to this
variegated mass of southern influences. If, further (the present
writer is already on record in support of this "if") the tale, however attenuated, however redone by the relay of local narrators,
passed to America, there to be worked into the thesauri of the
peoples who encountered it — then there opens up a new culture
historical chapter of a sort.

---

* Uno Holmberg, in his Siberian Mythology (MYTHOLOGY
OF ALL RACES series; Boston 1927), gives an excellent though
succinct and popularized account of the pertinent motifs as they
occur in Eurasia. His analysis of origins and diffusions agrees
very considerably with Dragomanov's; yet nowhere have I found
any indication that Holmberg was aware of the much earlier
writer's study.

III

I have remarked that the tale takes its shape during a period of climax and death to one world and embryogenesis of
another. The centuries between Alexander the Great and the
disintegration of Imperial Rome have no parallel until modern
times; and this period, I would be bold to say, is the most important of all history for modern man to study. Conventional
history seemingly does not view it as a single period; part of
it the Biblical scholars term the "intertestamental" period,
which saw the writing of Old Testament aprocryphas and late
canonical books, the pseudepigraphas and much that has been
uncovered among the Dead Sea scrolls. The classicists speak
of that same period as the Hellenistic. These are but segments
of something much greater. The centuries I have bracketed
determine the first age of cosmopolitanism in human history,
the like of which has not occurred again until today. For the
first time, entire cultures which had taken centuries to mature
and become sophisticate, and to develop comprehensive world-
views (their mythologies — their <u>Weltanschauungen</u>) collided
at all facets; and had to learn, through conflict, compromise,
and reconciliation, that no one of them could prevail over the
other; that irreconcilabilities could only be accommodated.
Often they did not learn this with a full realization of what the
lesson was; but circumstance is the strongest of despots. Of
this was born syncretism; successful syncretisms are still
called Judaism, Christianity, Islam; less durable ones have
been called Manicheism, Mithraism, Zervanism. Contending
mythologies produced orthodoxies, heresies, ideologic perse-
cutions, churches; founders of sects who attempted to select
and amalgamate out of the contradictory materials all too
readily at hand; sects that were more or less ephemeral, having a heyday followed by oblivion. But they forced orthodoxies
into being, and then had their revenge; for those who conquered
them were permanently changed by contact with those they defeated; they even came to embody some of the very things that
the struggle was supposed to have obliterated. There is a lesson here for moderns.

Dragomanov's study concerns an aspect, a region, a period
of this great, secular process; a segment of it which is far less
known in English than it deserves to be. It is a part of the world

history which even the author of the study, and his colleagues of the 1890's, were in no position to appreciate in full, because their time was not ripe for it.

IV

"Über dem Berge sind auch Leute." Slavic, Finnish, Magyar intellectuals have taken part in the building of European culture. We are used to a Tchaikovsky, a Smetana, a Dvořak, Moszkowski, Liszt; also, to a Turgeniev, a Pushkin. But we only glimpse, if we see at all, a Madács, Kropotkin, Kron, Jireček, Vazov. Yet the heart of Europe is the Danube; and the lands of the Slavs are at once Europe's rampart, window, and gateway facing the pulsations of Asia. In Slavdom there are folklore and music, lyric and epic poetry; there are also social and political theory, historiography, philosophy. There are, then, patterns of culture, * configurations of its growth. ** Dragomanov's essay is that of a thorough European operating in the arena of the nineteenth century upon Irano-Chaldean thought-materials; which materials have imprinted themselves upon Occidentals in certain ways but upon more easterly-dwelling peoples in other ways; and these peoples live in a <u>Lebensraum</u> whence has sprung a biodynamic that has destroyed empires and built cultural history.

V

Mixailo Dragomanov was born in 1841 at Gadač", in the Poltava district. He completed his university course at Kiev in 1863; specialized in and wrote on Roman History, 1864-1869. In 1875 he went to Geneva, and spent a number of years writing voluminously in political sociology. His theories had in mind particularly the problems of his native land; so that Ukrainians regard him as an "ideological founder" of modern Ukraine. In 1886 he returned to Kiev; in 1889 he accepted the chair of

---

* Benedict
** Kroeber

universal history in the University of Sofia, Bulgaria; he died in that city in 1895.

We may only surmise why he buried this important essay in the Bulgarian language. In the nineteenth century, Slavs had become very conscious of the close resemblances between their several languages, and the ancient common cultural heritage which those seemed to imply. The Pan-Slavic movement is a matter of history. The last Christian member of the family to become liberated from the Moslem yoke had been Bulgaria, in 1879. By 1889, the nation had a university and an Academy of Sciences, with an organ of publication. Dragomanov's scholarship was an earnest of excellence in the infant university. Bulgarian writers had been vigorously building a literature for a number of decades: the language was to take its place in the cultural concert of Europe. But the language has never become important. The scholarly excellence in the publications of the Academy* — and it is genuine — remains closed to all but a few non-Bulgarians.

Dragomanov belonged to a breed of men peculiar to nineteenth century Europe; they include Comte, J. S. Mill, Virchow, Lombroso, and many more of the ilk. Intellectuals, we might say, who could beat their pens into broadswords; who could theorize, then apply their theories to public affairs, and take enormous risks. Their day and place explain them.

With the Napoleonic convulsion, Europe left behind plum-colored knee-breeches, handicrafts, and the Age of Reason, and moved into an age of soot, industry, science, and sociologic ideologies. Power lodged in the middle class; the intellectual who would exploit and mobilize society's resources must either be born into that class or enter it by adaptation and adoption — either moving up or moving down.

Those intellectuals were a peculiarly hard-headed kind of idealist. They believed themselves realists, which in a way they were. In philosophy they tended to become positivists; anti-clerical, analytic to the point of atomism, seeking a whole in terms of the sum of its parts; public-minded and patriotic under their own interpretation of those terms. They saw people

---

* I am referring to publications prior to the 1930's. I am not familiar with the more recent literature.

first, not dynasties and churches; but societies rather than individuals. Institutions they looked upon as instruments for furthering the welfare of society and ethos; societies summarized, climactically, as nations. The intellectuals were versatile and indefatigable, with their own code of <u>noblesse oblige</u>. If today folklore, the ethnology of peasants, and sociology are dignified disciplines in state-maintained European universities, while their scope and aims do not coincide with what comes under these words in American universities, it is largely because in this country we have had another brand of intellectuals.

But if, some day, a culture-historian should undertake to study those Europeans as a culture phenomenon, he must not stop with the world of English, French, German, Italian; he must seek out the languages of Slavs, Magyars, Finns, and read their Dragomanovs. Über dem Berge sind auch Leute.

A note about the translations. Beside standard Bulgarian, they range over a number of Slavic languages and dialects and centuries. These have created difficulties; and I gladly acknowledge, with thanks, the helpful and gracious criticisms of Professor Oleg Maslennikov, of the Slavic Department of the University of California (Berkeley) and of Professor Albert B. Lord of the Department of Slavic Languages and Literatures of Harvard University. None the less, circumstances have forced the translations to be my own, and I must absorb any inaccuracies which the more versed may find. For the purposes of this translation, however, I am confident that no serious harm has been done. At one place I have taken the liberty of translating in full from Radloff a most remarkable tale which Dragomanov abbreviates, and substituting it.

And admittedly, were Veselovskij's <u>Razyskanija</u>, so often cited by Dragomanov, to have been translated from the Russian and placed beside the present work, the intelligibility of the latter would have been enhanced. However — μηδὲν ἄγαν.

Earl W. Count

Hamilton College
Clinton, New York

1 Two Bulgarian variants of the tale of the creation
of the world. — The Ukrainian variant. — Two
Ukrainian Christmas carols on cosmogony. — The
distribution of tales similar to the Bulgarian in Europe and Asia. — Earlier attempts at explaining the
origin of these tales: Erben, Afanasiev'' et al.; Alexander Veselovskij, Sumcov'' et al.; the observations
of Léger and the pamphlet of de Charencey; our attempt in the journal <u>Melusine</u>. — The recent monographs of Veselovskij. — A more exacting method is
indispensible: attention must be paid not only to the
similarities but to the differences in the tales as well,
and likewise to the conditions of origin, beginning
with the geographic. — The utter dissimilarities in
the cosmogonic tales of the Finnish Kalevala and of
the American and Oceanian myth tales from the main
mass of the European and Asiatic dualistic tales.
The oceanic character of the latter and the impossi-
bility of their basis having taken shape in the areas of
the Turks and Slavs.

One of the most interesting Bulgarian legends, in its basic
theme and its details, is that of the world-creation done by God
and the Devil together. There are two variants of it in print.
One, which is very detailed, was first issued in the publication
Obšt Trud II (1868): 73-78; later this was reprinted as an
appendix to our anthology <u>Malorusskija narodnyja predanija i
raskazy;</u>[1] and finally in the B<u>ạlgarska Xristomatija</u>[2] by Vazov
and Veličkov (pp. 46-49).

We shall be compelled to turn repeatedly to this remarkable
tale, which contains the whole book of Genesis in apocryphal
form and part of the Gospel; so we shall reproduce it here entire:

>   At first there was no earth and no people. Every-
> where was water. There were only the Lord and the
> devil, who at that time lived together.
>   Once the Lord said to the devil: "Let us make the
> earth and people."
>   "Let us do so," answered the devil, "but where
> shall we get dirt?"
>   "There is dirt under the water," said the Lord;
> "go down and get some."

"All right," answered the devil.

" But before you go down," said the Lord to the devil, " say: 'With God's power and mine!' Then you will reach bottom and find dirt."

The devil went down, but he did not say first, " With God's power and mine!" but: " With my power and God's power!" Therefore he did not reach bottom. The second time he did the same and again he did not reach bottom. Finally the third time he said, " With God's power and mine!" and then he reached bottom and with his nails he grasped a little dirt. That dirt the Lord put on the water and it became a little dry land.

When the devil saw that, he thought up this piece of deceit: he proposed that they sleep; then, when the Lord had fallen asleep, he would push him into the water, and thus he (the devil) would be left alone, and he could take credit for having made the earth. The Lord knew this, but he lay down and pretended to sleep. Then the devil got up, took the Lord in his hands, and started for the water, to throw him in. He walked towards the water, but the earth grew. As he did not reach the water he turned in the other direction, but again he did not reach the water. Then he turned in the third direction and when he again did not reach the water, he put the Lord down and lay down also. When he had slept a bit, it occurred to him that there was still a fourth direction. He picked up the Lord and carried him down toward the water, but still he could not reach it.

Then the devil roused the Lord: " Get up, Lord, let us bless the earth! Look how it has grown while we were sleeping."

" When you were carrying me in all four directions, to throw me into the water, and made a cross with me, I blessed the earth," said the Lord.

The devil got mad at this, left the Lord and ran away from him.

When the Lord was left alone and the earth had grown so big that the sun could not cover it, he created in spirit angels and sent an expedition of angels to call the devil and ask him what to do to make the earth stop growing.

At that time the devil created the goat, and, as he was coming to the Lord, he straddled the billy and gave him a bridle made of a leek; from then on goats have had beards.

When the angels saw the devil riding a billy, they laughed at him, and he became angry and went back.

Immediately the Lord created the bee and said to her: "Go quickly and alight on the devil's shoulder and listen to what he says; then come and tell me."

The bee went off, lit on the devil's shoulder, and he was saying, "Huh, what a stupid Lord! He does not know enough to take a stick and make the sign of a cross to the four directions and say, 'That is enough earth,' but instead he wonders what to do!" When the bee heard that, she buzzed and flew from his shoulder. The devil turned, saw her, and exclaimed: "Let him eat your excrement, whoever sent you!"

When she came to the Lord, the bee told him that the devil had said, "Huh, what a stupid Lord! He does not know enough to take a stick and make the sign of a cross over the earth in the four directions and say, 'That is enough earth,' but instead he wonders what to do." — "And as for me," said the bee, "he said: 'Let him eat your increment, whoever sent you!'"

The Lord did this and the earth stopped growing. To the bee he said, "From now on let there be no excrements sweeter than yours!"

After this the Lord made a man from mud, and from him people multiplied on the earth; and when they began to die the Lord summoned the devil and invited him to live with him. The devil agreed, but on this condition: that the living people belong to the Lord, but the dead ones be his. The Lord agreed to this; and that they might (not?)[3] die soon, he made them live 200 or 300 years.

After much time, when the Lord saw that the dead were becoming more numerous than the living, and that the devil had more people than he did, he wanted to rescind the contract, but did not know how. Therefore he asked some of his people, like Abraham, Moses, and Joseph ("Jusup"); he asked even the angels, but no one could advise him how to rescind the contract. They began to ask the devil about it, and once one of the Lord's people asked him, "Since you have made a contract with the Lord that the living shall be his and the dead yours, can the Lord rescind the contract?" "The Lord cannot do it alone," answered the devil, "but his son could, if only he could have a son born of his spirit and not as other people are made."

When they told this to the Lord, he began to think: "How can a son be born to me on the earth, before all men, from my spirit only?" He thought and he thought, and could not figure it out. Therefore once he himself asked the devil, "How can I have a son born of my

spirit?" "Very easily," responded the devil. "Make
a bouquet of flowers of hyssop, put it in your bosom,
sleep with it one night while you keep thinking that
you wish a son to be born from the spirit of God; and
when you get up, send it to the devout and virgin Mary,
sister of Jordan, and let her smell it, and she will
become pregnant." The Lord did as the devil told
him and sent the hyssop bouquet by the angel Gabriel
to the Virgin Mary. And the angel said to her, "I
bring you from God a gift of lovely flowers; smell it,
and see how lovely it smells." She took the bouquet
and smelled it. After two or three days Mary became
pregnant.

Once Mary with her brother Jordan started for
church; and as they approached the church Jordan
began to think on how people would laugh at him as
he walked with his sister, she still unmarried and yet
pregnant; so he said to her, "Wait here a bit, sister.
I am going back home, and I'll come again right
away." He went home, got on his horse, and took
up his lance; and when he had come to his sister Mary,
he speared her above the breast. She took hold of his
spear, drew it from her breast and said to him, "Wait,
brother, let me wipe off your spear, so that people
will not accuse you of having speared me!" And with
the skirt of her dress she wiped off the blood.

Then Jordan fled; but from Mary's wound that
was made above her breast by her brother's lance,
was Jesus Christ born, of the spirit of God; so Mary
still remained a virgin.

When the Lord heard that Jesus Christ had been
born, he ordered that after 33 years he should be
christened.

Jordan fled to far places, and after a long time,
when he heard from people what a miracle of God had
befallen his sister Mary, he returned home and begged
his sister to forgive him. She said to him, "Since you
acknowledge that you have sinned, cut off the hand with
which you pierced me; then I will forgive you." He
cut off his hand, therefore he became a holy man.

Jesus Christ entered God's place and said to the
devil, "I am going to take from you the dead people,
that they may all become mine." "How will you do
that," answered the devil, "when I have the contract
with your father that the living shall be his and the
dead mine!" "You have a contract with my father,
but not with me," Jesus told him. The devil could do
nothing — he had tricked himself.

And thus the companionship of God and the devil

was completely destroyed, which companionship had
lasted 800,000 years from the creation of the world
to the birth of Jesus Christ.

When Christ had taken from him the dead people,
the devil instructed the Jews not to believe him in
anything. The Jews listened to the devil and began
to hunt for Christ to kill him. When they could not
find him because they did not know him, they proposed to one of his servants, Judas, that he betray
him. Judas said to them, "You come to a certain
place with me, where Christ will be also, and I will
begin to pour wine to him and the apostles. I will
cough and turn toward you; you will know that that is
Christ; jump in and grab him."

Judas betrayed Christ, but he knew that he would
resurrect; therefore he went and hanged himself so
that when Christ should come to rescue the dead from
Hades, he would save him along with the others. But
by the time that Judas had hanged himself and gone to
Hell, Christ had risen and rescued the dead from it,
and Judas had not yet gotten there; so he was left
there alone in Hell.

A less full variant of this tale has been printed by Mr. Drinov in the Periodičesko Spisanie na Bəlgarskoto Knižovno
Družestvo vol. VIII, 1884, in the Records of Nešo Bončov,
pp. 124-126. Unfortunately, the whole tale has been taken down
with but incomplete success from the mouth of someone who
obviously had not mastered its content thoroughly; yet we find
in it some interesting details which are especially important
for determining the relationship of the Bulgarian tale to those
of other countries.

Here is this variant:

According to what old folks tell, the devil once
had equal power with God, for God asked his advice
in many things. And as to where the devil came from,
this is what they have told me. The Lord ("Dedo
Gospod") used to take a walk on mountains and plains,
and was really happy; but still he was not quite con-
tented because he did not have a companion to talk
with and to pass the time away with merrily. Once
as he was walking he noticed his shadow, and he
cried to it, "Arise, comrad!" And the shadow rose
up before him, like a man; but it was not a man, but
the devil. From then on the Lord had him for a com-
rade and the devil became his friend. The Lord was

awfully pleased with the comradeship of this companion and therefore he wanted to reward the devil with whatever he should desire. The devil wanted them to divide the world in half. "Let the earth be mine, and the heaven yours," said the devil, "and let us divide up the people: you take the living, and give me the dead ones." "So let it be, as you say," the Lord responded. "All right," said the devil, "But give me a receipt to confirm the matter." A receipt was made and given the devil.

When Grandpa Adam was driven out of paradise, God gave him land, to work it freely. Once the devil, when he had climbed onto a large rock to look around over the land, spied Adam and Grandma Eve plowing. He rushed down at them and cried out with his big voice, "How dare you plow this land without asking the proprietor?" "But we are plowing with his permission," said they. "I am the proprietor. You did not ask me, did you? Leave the land alone, and from now on let no one dare touch it!" When God learned about this, he was very sorry and he began to reproach himself for ever having given the devil a receipt.

When the people had multiplied, the devil plagued the righteous along with the evil ones. Therefore God began to think of taking the power away from the devil. He called the Angel, asked him what he thought should be done, and then asked him if he thought he could get the receipt away from the devil. The Angel thought a bit, then said he could. And so the Angel went to the devil in the form of a man, and proposed to serve him for a few years; but secretly he had the purpose of getting away the receipt. The devil from the beginning took a fancy to the Angel; but no matter how much he confided in him, he always hid the receipt.

Once they were walking by a lake, and the Angel asked, "Can you bring out a handful of sand from the bottom of the lake? You are stronger and cleverer than I, but you can't do it, and I can." "Well, let's see," said the devil.

The Angel stripped, immediately threw himself into the water, and right away he showed himself at the surface with sand in his fist. The devil, to show that he was not inferior, undressed, plunged into the water, but remembered that his receipt was left in his shirt, and it might fall into the hands of his companion, so he returned when he had gone only half-way; he looked — nothing of the sort! Again he dived but came back, up to three times. At last when he was certain that his companion had nothing to do with the receipt, he went clear to the bottom without misgivings. It was easy for the devil to sink, but to come up was a bit hard, because he is a devil and a devil is heavy; how could he compete in <u>lightness</u> with an angel? And while he was delaying in the water, the Angel got out the receipt and flew towards heaven. The devil took after him and caught up just as he was entering heaven, grabbed him with his nails and tore off a piece of flesh from his sole, but still he could not pull him back, as the Angel was already with God. The devil went back, his powers fell away, and from then on he became an enemy of God. When the Angel came before God with the receipt he was limping in his left foot, and he complained to God that the devil had deformed his foot. "Never mind," said the good Lord (Dedo Gospod) to him, "I will make all people like that, so you need not be embarrassed." Since then our soles have been hollowed.

Even before the Bulgarian tales just adduced had appeared, some of their details were known from the oral literature of the various eastern European peoples — the Russians, the Finns, and some Turkic tribes. That the Bulgarian reader may compare them with the Bulgarian variants known up to now, we shall for the present adduce but one tale: a Ukrainian, which is printed in the periodical <u>Osnova</u> vol. VI (1861): 59-60, and in our "Maloruski Predanija i Raskazi" pp. 88-92 (translated into German in the <u>Zeitschrift für deutsche Mythologie</u> vol. IV: 157-158).

THE CREATION AND BLESSING OF THE WORLD
(BY GOD AND SATANAIL)

When the Lord had thought of creating the world, he said to the oldest angel, Satanail:
"What say you to our going and creating the world?"
"Let us do so, God," answered Satanail.
And so they went to the sea; and such a dark sea, it is said, so abysmal! Then said the Lord to Satanail,
"Do you see," says he, "this abyss?"
"I see it, God."
"Go," says he, "into the very bottom of this abyss, and bring me a handful of sand. Only be careful, when you take it, to say to yourself, 'I take you, earth, in the name of the Lord.'"

"All right, God."

Satanail dived into the abyss even to the sand, but he became provoked.

"No, God," says he, "I will add on my own name; let it be at one and the same time for you and for me!" — He took the sand and said, "I take you, earth, in the name of the Lord and in mine." He said it and he said it. Time came to take out the sand, but, low and behold, the water washes it from his hand; he squeezes his handful — but how can you deceive God? When he came back out of the water, there was no sand in his hand; the water had washed it out.

"Don't try deceit, Satanail," says the Lord. "Go again, but don't add on your own name."

Satanail went again, but a devil is always a devil; again he said, "I take you, earth, in the name of the Lord and in mine!" And again there remained no sand in his hand.

The third time Satanail finally said, "I take you, earth, in the name of the Lord!" And only then was he able to bring it back, without squeezing his hand: thus he carried it in his hand, hoping (now) that the water would wash it away, but in vain: as he had filled his hand, so he brought it to God.

The Lord took this sand, started over the sea and scattered it, and Satanail licked his hand: "I'll save a grain for myself," he thought, "and after that I'll make an earth myself!" And the Lord scattered the sand.

"Well, now," says he, "Satanail, is there no more sand?"

"No more, God!"

"Then it must be blessed!" said the Lord; and he blessed the earth in the four directions; and when he had blessed it, it began to grow.

The earth grew, but that in the devil's mouth grew too, and it grew so much that the mouth of the devil began to swell. Then God said, "Spit, Satanail!" He began to spit and hawk; and where he spat, there grew mountains; and where he hawked, there grew rocks. This is why the earth is not flat. They say also that no one knows how much these rocks and mountains might have grown if Peter and Paul had not cursed them, so they do not grow any more.

The Lord said then to Satanail, "Now," said he, "Satanail, it still remains to dedicate the earth; but let it grow, while we rest."

"All right, God," said Satanail.

And they lay down to rest. The Lord slept, and

Satanail pondered on how to drown the Lord and grab the earth for himself. He picked up the Lord and hurried with him towards the sea. He ran half a day; there was ever no sea; it became midnight; still no sea. He ran to all four quarters of the earth — nowhere did he find sea; of course, the earth had grown so much already that its edges touched the heaven, so where would you expect to find sea? He saw that he could do nothing; he carried God back to the same place and lay down beside him. He lay a while and then he roused God:

"Get up, God," says he, "and let's dedicate the earth!"

But God said to him, "Don't worry, Satanail. My earth is dedicated; this night I dedicated it in all four quarters!"

The larger part of the tales known to date and having such content, recorded among the various Slavic and non-Slavic peoples from the Adriatic to the Yakutsk territory, resemble considerably the Bulgarian and Ukrainian variants. We observe sharper divergences only in the Little-Russian Christmas carols, which also tell of the world-creation. In one of them appear as creators of the world the Lord and the apostles Peter and Paul, who here replace the devil in the tales adduced above:

As it was ages ago,
Before the world began,
There lapped the blue sea;
On the blue sea
Stood three plane-trees,
On the three plane-trees three doves:
On the first dove
Sat the Lord himself,
On the other dove
Sat St. Peter,
On the third dove
Sat St. Paul.
The Lord said to St. Peter
"Dive, Peter, to the bottom of the sea,
Fetch, Peter, the yellow sand,
And carry it throughout the world.
Create, Peter,
Heaven and earth,
Heaven with the stars,
Earth with the flowers."

>Peter dived and did not reach bottom,
>And did not fetch sand,
>And did not scatter it over the world,
>And Peter did not create
>Heaven and earth,
>Neither heaven with the stars,
>Nor earth with the flowers.

(The same is repeated with St. Paul.)

>There dived the Lord himself to the bottom of the sea,
>The Lord fetched yellow sand,
>And scattered it throughout the world,
>The Lord himself created
>Heaven and earth,
>Heaven with the stars,
>Earth with the flowers.

(A. Nowosielski, Lud Ukrainski I. 103-104). In another Christmas carol, recorded in Galicia, the role of the Creator is taken by the three doves:

>When there was in the beginning no world,
>Then there was neither heaven nor earth,
>Everywhere was a blue sea,
>And in the medst of the sea a green plane-tree,
>On the plane-tree three doves,
>Three doves take counsel,
>Take counsel as to how to create the world.
>"Let us plunge to the bottom of the sea,
>Let us gather fine sand;
>Let us scatter fine sand,
>That it may become for us black earth.
>Let us get golden rocks,
>Let us scatter golden rocks,
>Let there be for us a bright sky,
>A bright sky, a shining sun,
>A shining sun and a bright moon,
>A bright moon, a bright morning-star,
>A bright morning-star and little starlets.[4]

The text of this Christmas carol has been translated into French by Xodzko, in Contes des paysans et des pâtres slaves. (Paris, 1864, p. 374.)

Slavic tales of this sort have long drawn the attention of Slavic scholars, and according to the opinions which until recently have prevailed among these, the tales are to be explained as ramains of ancient Slavic dualism: the belief in Belbog and

Chernobog (Cf. especially Erben: Báje slovenské stvoření světa, in Časopise Musea Království českého; 1866, p. 35f; and Afanazjev: Poětičeskija vozzrenija Slavjan''na prirodu; 1868, v. II:458f.).

Some of the similarities between the tales adduced above and the Slavic written apocryphas have been considered as confirmation of these opinions, since the Slavic scholars at one time looked upon the apocryphas themselves as the product of hybrid belief; as a mixture of Christianity with the Slavic ethnic beliefs. That similar tales existed among the Finnic and Turkic peoples did not bother the Slavic scholars in the least, since they looked upon the tales of their fellow-kinsmen as remnants of the original Slavic mythology.

With the application of the comparative method to the ethnic variants and traditions, and with the appearance of the "theory of borrowing," even in the Slavic scholarship, the opinions of Erben, Afanasiev et al. finally had to meet refutation. The younger scholars began to seek other, foreign sources for the Slavic dualistic tales of the world-creation.

First of all Prof. Alexander Veselovskij expressed himself in this spirit; in his essay, Slavjanskija skazanija o Solomoně i Kitovrasě (1872), he notes in passing that "the folk tales recorded in Russia and Bulgaria about the dualistic world-creation derive from the written Bogomil apocryphas, in which have been reflected eastern religious conceptions" (op. cit. p. 164).

This opinion as to the Gnostic-Iranian-Syrian provenience of the Slavic dualistic tales of the world-creation, through the medium of the Bogomils, was expressed also by Sumcov'' in his Očerki istorii južnorusskix apokrifičeskix skazanii i pesen' (Kievska Starina; 1887, June-July, pp. 255f). But Sumcov'' does not pursue the matter in detail, and he does not reject from the tales which concern us the presence of some ancient Slavic religio-mythic element. Besides, Sumcov'' adduces at the beginning of his article (from the citations of Reville, Les religions des peuples non civilisés, I:282) a North American tale: how the various animals at the command of the "Great Spirit" extracted from the water parts of the earth. Sumcov'' finds in this tale resemblances to the similar Ukrainian; but he does not assume the burdensome task of comparing extensively the Slavic tales of this sort with those of other tribes; he confines himself merely to expressing "amazement at the fact that there exist such similar tales among peoples separated by vast distances and who never have been in contact with each other."

Among the non-Slavic scholars, Léger is the first to concern himself with our dualistic tales, in his short but valuable article on the Slavic mythology, printed first in the Revue historique des religions, and later in Nouvelles études slaves, 2-me série.

On the whole, Léger does not agree with Erben's ideas about the primeval Slavic dualism, which according to the opinion of the Czech scholar is supposed to be reflected also in the tales that concern us. A propos of the latter, Léger says: "The learned orientalist, Joseph Deremberg, assures me that the larger part of this tale must be sought for in the Midrash, i. e., in the legendary traditions which the folk (?) imagination had added to the sacred text (of the Bible). Unfortunately, the text of the Midrash is accessible, at least for the present, only to the professional Hebraists. Thus it transpires that the legends on which Erben bases are of Semitic, Christian, or Manichean provenience, and by no means Slavic." (op. cit. 200-201).

Unfortunately, Deremberg even to the present has not indicated in print what these tales from the Midrash are that parallel our own: although we challenged him directly to do so, in Mélusine #10 (1888). In the translations from the Talmudic literature (the Midrash belongs to this), which have appeared in the more accessible languages, we find nothing like our legends.

After Léger, the Slavic tales of the world-creation drew the attention of the French Americanist De Charencey in his pamphlet, Une légende cosmogonique (Havre, Imprimerie Lepelletier, 1884). It turns out that this scholar was aware of the Galician Christmas carol of the doves, adduced above, the Galician variant of the dualistic legend, and a fragment of the Slavic apocryphal book about God and Satan on the Tiberian sea which was adduced by Pypin in his Istorija na Slavjanskitě Literaturi, in the chapter on the Bulgarians; for which reason De Charencey calls it a "Bulgarian legend." These Slavic stories the French Americanist sets beside a considerable number of legends from the Old and the New World, and concentrates upon the Vogul and American tales.

De Charencey divides all these stories into three circles:
(1) A Continental version, distributed over both New and

Old Worlds, in which the earth is represented as drawn up out
of the sea by some animate being (mammal or bird);

(2) An insular version, peculiar to Japan and the Poly-
nesian islands, in which God himself extracts the earth out of
the water, like some fish, with fishing-tackle or a stick;

(3) An (East) Indian or mixed version, which has been
formed by the fusion of the other two.

De Charencey considers the insular as being the oldest. [5]
The Slavic tales he counts with the continental.

In 1888 we inserted in the French journal of folklore Mélusine (##9 and 10) the first Bulgarian legend we have adduced
here, and we accompanied it with some explanations, in which
we tried to survey in detail, even if concisely, the composition
of the Bulgarian dualistic legend, attempting to show both its
resemblance to other like tales as well as its differences. We
supposed that its base came out of Asia, on the shores of the
Indian Ocean; that afterwards it was altered in the Babylonian
and Iranian medium, until it had received with slight alterations
the form under which it diffused via the Manicheanising preach-
ers into Northern Asia and Eastern Europe.

In 1889 Mochul'skij printed in the Russkij Filologičeskij
Věstnik" an article that is interesting in many connections: Za
mnimija dualizm" v slavjanskata mitologija, in which he sub-
mits to skeptical criticism the general hypotheses anent the
existence of dualism in the Slavic tribal mythology. The dualistic elements, which are observed in the various mediaeval Slavic
beliefs and in the oral literature of today, Močul'skij derives
from sources among other tribes, predominantly Iranian. Unfortunately, Močul'skij did not tarry long to acquaint himself
thoroughly with the beliefs of the eastern tribes and of Gnosticism; and, at variance with the basic general hypotheses furnished us by the comparative history of religions, he ascribes
monotheism, instead of dualism, to the proto-Slavs. Furthermore, the destructive criticism of Močul'skij and his conception of the Slavic oral dualistic legends as derived from the
written apocryphas that are saturated with Iranian ideas, are
in our opinion poorly founded. [6]

Recently, Alexander Veselovskij has devoted to our legends
two special monographs: Dualističeskija poverija o mirozdanii
(Razyskanija v oblasti russkago duxovnago stixa XI-XVII, (1889):
XI: 1-116) and "Eščo po voprosu o dualitičeskix kosmogonijax

(Razyskanija etc. XVIII-XXIV (1891):XX, 105-136; but first of
all in Etnografičeskoe Obozrenie).

In the first of these monographs Veselovskij strongly departs from his earlier opinion as to the Irano-Gnostic provenience of the Slavic dualistic legends, and approaches the opinion
of the Finnish scholar Julian Kron (I. Kron: Finska literaturens
historia); namely, that the base of these stories was elaborated
by the Finno-Magyar or Ural-Altaic tribes (Razyskanija XI: 4).
Veselovskij disagrees with Kron only in details; but in the end
he admits the possibility that Gnosticism has influenced these
Finnic legends as they traveled southward, that is, toward the
Slavs, and vice versa — from the south northward, from the
Slavs to the Finns and the Ural-Altaians.

Unfortunately, Veselovskij expresses the latter assumption
a bit obscurely.[7] Besides, he has not attempted to show, no
matter how essential the matter be, the consequences of this
double movement in the case of the variants before us; consequences which should be visible if the movement itself had existed.

The investigation of Veselovskij provokes, among other
things, the observation on the part of the editor of Russkaja
Mysl' (July 1890), that perhaps in the dualistic legends of the
various peoples we have to do with independent geneses of one
and the same conception in various mutually separate ethnic
spheres, and that perhaps dualism is one of the steps in the
religious development of many peoples.[8]

This remark, plus the material collected, whether new and
unknown, or whether released in his first investigation, led
Veselovskij to write his second monograph on our subject: "Eščo
o dualističeskix kosmogonijax," in which, among other things,
he turns his attention also to the cosmogonic legends of the
American peoples; these, according to Veselovskij, may be
taken as dualistic and be compared to the legends of the Old
World that had been the subject of his first study. In this new
investigation of his, the learned St. Petersburg academician
almost completely repudiates the "Finnic theory," to which he
had adhered in his first monograph.

Adducing a trans-Caucasian, Suanitian legend (we shall
observe here à propos, that it is strikingly like the Bulgarian),
Veselovskij says: "The Suanitian cosmogonic legend does not
take us outside the boundaries of its geographic distribution in

Europe as assumed by us; its Christian motifs contribute nothing new to the solution of the problem: What ethnic-religious faith has entered into the base of the story of the two brother creators, God and Satanail? [9]   I had assumed that it is not Aryan but Turco-Finnic; this view the Finnic (in the broad sense) and Turkic variants of the cosmogonic legend might have supported, in which as yet no influence of Christianity (Bogomilism) can be observed. But I know of no such variants; my attempt to uncover the dualistic currents in the cosmogony of the Kalevala were stimulated by the conviction that the dualism in the legends of the world-creation known to us can not be explained exclusively through the Iranian conceptions which are manifest in the historical forms of Bogomilism." [10]

Veselovskij finds "indirect confirmation of this opinion in the conceptions of the North American Hurons, Iroquois, and Algonkins about the two brother demiurges, the representatives of the good and bad beginning"; and thereupon he presents the American legends, which he considers to be almost identical with the Finnic, Turkic, and Slavic.

Otherwise, our author does not draw from this assumed similarity any decisive conclusion, but merely declares that his "explanation of the Slavic, Finno-Turkic, and American dualistic myth often has led him to the thought expressed by the editor of the 'Russkaja Mysl''; namely, that perhaps we have here to do with the independent genesis of one and the same conception in different ethnic spheres which have never been in contact. . . . To demonstrate this in connection with the cosmogonic myth we have analyzed, must be the work of some future investigator; up to now I have refrained from expressing this assumption, first, because the question of independent genesis can be posed only when the other question has been answered in the negative: Was it possible for human groups which brought, for instance, nephrite to Mexico — a thing otherwise not found in America — in very early prehistoric times, to have intercommunicated? For why not then also fragments of the myth? " (Razyskanija XX:123).

In this manner Veselovskij eschews categorically the attempt to explain theoretically the evolution of the dualistic beliefs which have occupied him — even though he has accumulated a huge mass of material that misses completeness only by the absence of the Hindu and Syro-Mesopotamian. These

latter indeed are very important stories, as we shall try to
show later on.

We think, moreover, that this result of Veselovskij's investigation, which is negative in its theoretical aspect, is due
not only to the lack of the just-mentioned Hindu-Mesopotamian
legends, but also to his method not being strict enough.

The comparative investigation of the stories must have in
mind not only the similarities in their bases, but also similarities and differences in their details.

Beside this, when it is a question of the original kinship
of some story and the alterations of form which it has under-
gone in its movements throughout various regions, one must
pay particular attention to the various conditions of origin,
beginning with the geographical. Only in this way can we determine the genesis of the stories which we find among the
various peoples, and indicate their true kinship, and thus also
separate the indigenous stories of a given region from those
that have been borrowed.

If with such methodological postulates we turn to the tales
of the Finnish Kalevala and the American tales which Veselovskij
has reviewed, we shall see that these tales have to be detached
completely from the dualistic legends, which — ranging from
the Bulgarian to the Siberian, Turkic, and Yakut — represent
truly a progeny that inevitably must have proceeded from one
common ancestor.

The common basis of the tales in this family is this: the
antagonism of two divine individuals at the creation of the world,
of whom the one despatches the other into the water to fetch a
portion of the matter from which to create dry land.

In the tales of the Kalevala, such a plot is quite lacking.[11]
In the tales of creation by Veinamoinen and Ilmerinen there is
no antagonism; and later they create a wonderful spring (Samno),
and not dry land; at which task Ilmerinen works under Veinamoinen's orders honestly and without a thought of deceiving
him, as for instance Satanail in the Bulgarian, Ukrainian etc.,
tales.

In the 37th rune, which Veselovskij places beside an Altaian story that essentially resembles the Slavic, there is but
one point of similarity with these: where Ilmerinen extracts
from the sea the matter for creation; but this matter is gold
and silver, and the object of creation itself is a woman, whom

Ilmerinen wished to have in place of another he had lost; this
is thoroughly different from the object in the Turkic and Slavic
stories.

The process of creation (forgoing) is also quite different.

The "diving" to the bottom of the sea, in another episode
of the Kalevala, on which diving Veselovskij insists, likewise
has nothing in common with the creation by Satanail. In the
Kalevala "a blue duck, at the command of Veinamöinen, dives
into the sea to fetch from it the tears of the skilled singer and
demiurge" (Razyskanija XI:108-109).

Such "divings" can be found by the tens in various stories
which have nothing in common with the dualistic legends of the
creation of the world.

Even if the shooting by the cross-eyed Lapp at Veinamöinen
represents, as reconstructed by Lönrot, a remnant of cosmogonic dualism, it still remains without analogy with the details of
the Slavic tales about God and Satanail.

Examples of such shootings are likewise numerous in all
sorts of mutually quite different stories and mythologies.

In some North American traditions of the creation of the
world there is more similarity to the Slavic dualistic legends;
nevertheless these traditions also must be placed in the cate-
gory of completely independent tales.

Certain other North American traditions, it is true, treat
of the world-creation out of a substance obtained by "diving";
but strictly speaking here too there is nothing dualistic. Thus,
for instance, the Tacullies of Britich Columbia tell that at first
there existed in the world only water and the muskrat. The
latter dived to the bottom of the water to seek food, and there
filled its mouth with slime. The animal spat out this slime and
thus, little by little, an island was formed, which, as it expanded, became the earth, i. e., dry land.[12]

Here, of course, we find some traits known to us from the
Slavic legends; but the legend itself, and especially the dualistic antagonism of the demiurges, we do not find.

Thus likewise we must admit the distinctiveness of the
Slavic and other American tales and legends like them, from
those which De Charencey terms insular. These latter, in
which God extracts the earth (the already-formed islands) out
of the water, like a fish, by means of tackle, contain nothing
dualistic, and neither in their plot nor their details do

they present anything similar to the Slavic legends known to us.[13]

The major number of the American legends likewise contain no dualism whatever, particularly in the sense of an antagonism between the demiurges, and their plots are completely different from those of the Slavic tales, so that they have strictly only the following two traits in common with the Slavic: the diving of a certain being into the water and the fetching of particles out of it, from which later the dry land is formed; i.e., traits which are quite inadequate for establishing a genetic connection between the American and the Slavic tales.

The American legends, which are summarized by Waitz, Reville, and Lang from the materials which had been supplied them by various travellers, reduce to the following: in the beginning of the world, when the creator (who is represented differently in the various tribes) is over the waters, he orders the different animals (which means those who exist along with him) to fetch from the bottom of the water the particles of land. The beaver dives to the bottom, but does not succeed. The muskrat, on the other hand, brings up one grain of earth, from which the creator by breathing on it makes the dry land.[14]

De Charencey adduces some more developed legends gathered from the various tribes of Canada on the St. Lawrence river. According to these legends, before the creation of the earth (the dry land) everything was covered with water. The creator (whom some of the tribes take to be their ancestor and call the Great Hare, even though they conceive him in human form)[15] floated upon the water along with various animals on a large raft. The Great Hare wished to stop the raft on something solid, but on the water he saw nothing but swans and other birds; and finally he sent a beaver to the bottom of the water to fetch some earth. The beaver hesitated, but then agreed, dived into the water and was gone for a long time; finally it emerged almost dead, and motionless. The other animals searched its tail, but found nothing. The same is repeated with the otter. Then the muskrat offered its services. Three times it dived without success; but after the fourth try the animals found under its claws a small grain of sand. The Great Hare threw this grain onto the raft and it began to grow. When it had reached the size of a mountain, the Great Hare decided to encircle it; but the mountain kept on growing. Then he ordered the fox to

travel over the dry land. The fox went, returned and said that
the dry land was already big enough to feed and contain all the
animals. But the Great Hare found that the dry land was not
yet big enough and began again to go around it, so as to enlarge
it; to this day he is still doing so. And'to this day, when the
Algonkins hear sounds in the forest, they say that the Great
Hare is enlarging the earth.[16]

In these tales likewise there is nothing like the dualism of
the Slavic and Turkic cosmogonic legends; even the two agents
are not presented in them.

We are in possession of one more North American (Iroquois-
Huron) cosmogonic legend, on which Veselovskij dwells particularly, placing it in connection with the Slavic and Turkic dualistic legends of the world-creation.[17] In this legend, printed in
the Journal of American Folklore I (1888): 180-183 (in the stories of Horatio Hale: Huron Folklore) we encounter also episodes
of obtaining the earth-particles from the water; but it is inserted
into the plot of a thoroughly peculiar theme:

> From the sky there came a divine woman, and
> two birds supported her on the water. These two birds
> thereupon called to their aid various other animals,
> of which the tortoise agreed to take the goddess on its
> back, then sent various animals into the depth of the
> water to fetch land from it. Out of this earth, which
> the goddess spread about the turtle, the dry land was
> formed. After this the woman gave birth to twins,
> the one good, the other bad, of whom the latter burst
> through his mother's groin and thus became the cause
> of her death. From the body of the woman there grew
> forth the plants useful to man, and after that the one
> twin created the things which are useful to man, while
> the other those which are harmful.

It is obvious that the diving into the water after earth is
here an added episode. The basis itself of the legend, even
though its ending is dualistic, has nothing in common with the
Slavic and other like legends about God and Satanail.

If it can be said of the preceding American legends that they
contain a diving for earth but lack dualism, for this one it can
be said that it contains dualism, but it is expressed and set quite
differently, and not at all as in the dualistic legends of the Old
World; and for this reason all these American legends can have
no genetic connection with the latter.

If we compare the cosmogonic legends set forth above with the life-environment of the tribes in which they have been recorded, we shall see that the oceanic character in the legends of the insular inhabitants of the Pacific Ocean, the Japanese and the Polynesians, completely correspond to the oceanic geography of the dwelling-place of these peoples, and therefore it was possible for these legends to appear autochthonously.

The same must be said of the legends of the North American tribes, which undoubtedly have lived on the shores of the ocean, and even today live in a region rich in bodies of water: between the Great Lakes and Hudson's Bay. Quite different is the geographic environment of the Slavs and the Turkic tribes, who consist of <u>continental</u> peoples. The oceanic cosmogonies which are found among them must inevitably be of foreign derivation, while on the other hand the resemblance of these cosmogonies, not only at base but in details, speaks for the presumption that the dualistic legends of the Slavs and the Turks, from Bulgaria to the Yakut country, must have proceeded from one source.

Let us try to determine this source.

Notes

1. Little-Russian National Traditions and Tales.

2. Bulgarian Chrestomathy.

3. Negative supplied by the translator. EWC

4. We adduce this Christmas carol after a variant that was printed first by Nowosielski in the <u>Dziennik Warszawski</u> (1854) #99, and later reprinted by Kohlberg in <u>Rokusie</u> I: 348-349, with the note that this variant was recorded by Vagilevič'' on the Dniestr. In the other variants there are a few differences: two doves, not three; two oaks instead of the plane trees; blue stone instead of gold; etc. Cf. Golovackij: <u>Pesni Galickoj i Ugorskoj Russi</u> II: 5, from the Sjanocki district; Potebin: <u>Ob''jasnenie malorusskix narodnyx pesen'</u> II: 738-739. It would be desirable to verify carefully and critically the several variants, so as to separate out their ethnic peculiarities from the corrections made by the editors. The oldest printed texts of this Christmas carol we find in Šafařik: <u>Slovanski narodopis</u> (1842): 117, with a citation to the Christmas carol recorded by Vagilevič'', though with some divergences from the text of Nowosielski; later, in <u>Majak''</u> XI: 56, in Kostomarov'': <u>Ob'' istorič. značenie russkoj nar.</u>

poèzii (1843): 66. According to Golovackij, after each verse of
the Christmas carols comes the refrain:

> Breathe, then, breathe, Lord,
> And with thy holy spirit upon the earth.

5. The chapter on this version is poorly developed in the
pamphlet of the French scholar.

6. One of the weakest sides of scholarship in Russia is
the general absence of a proper attention to the newest investigations among the western scholars in the area of the evolution
of religion.

7. Referring to the two theories for explaining the similarities of the beliefs and stories of the various peoples — the
theory of general common bases and the theory of borrowing,
and after remarking that neither of them is applicable separatim,
Veselovskij says, "The theory of borrowing presupposes the
theory of common bases, and vice versa; the analysis of every
fact of folklore must turn equally to the one and to the other
side of the question, since it is possible that the myths, the
tales, the songs have influenced each other reciprocally over
and over, and each time under new conditions, both in the
medium that appropriates them and in the material appropriated.
"The German epic motifs have entered into the base of the
French chansons de geste, and have recrossed the Rhine as
knightly and feudal poems. Instead of this coloring (query: what
coloring?), I assume a Christian-Bogomil one in these legends,
which have come to us southward from the north and again have
returned northward; thus coming one of those full circuits which
here is difficult to follow, yet which the investigator must always
have in mind as a possibility." (Razyskanija XI, 115-116).

8. Later on we shall discuss this question rather extensively; here let us note merely that dualism not only could have
been but actually was such a transitory stage everywhere; the
problem, however, is one of quality and quantity of dualism.
For instance, the dualistic features that are encountered in all
mythologies that tell of warring gods are one thing; quite another is the dualism that is catechetic and consequently is
dragged through the tiniest of trivialia, as in the Zend-Avesta
and other Iranian books.

9. Further along we shall demonstrate in how far the
Transcaucasian variants of the dualistic cosmogony legend can
shed light on the problem of the region where the legend ac-
quired the shapes under which it moved on to the Slavs.

10. Razyskanija etc. XX: 117.

11. We feel we must caution that a strictly scholarly analysis of the Kalevala is impossible, since the Finnish poem is not a single body of raw material but a collection of various separate tales brought together from a variety of places by Lönrot.

12. Andrew Lang, <u>Myth, Ritual and Religion</u> I: 191-192; idem, <u>La Mythologie</u>, trad. par L. Parmentier 164.

13. De Charencey, op. cit. 36-42.

14. Waitz: <u>Anthropologie der Naturvölker</u> III: 183-184; Reville: <u>Les religions des peuples non civilisés</u> I: 282; A. Lang: <u>Myth, Ritual and Religion</u> I: 182.

15. De Charencey says that the name of this Great Hare — Manibojo, Nanabojou, Michabo, Messou — means Great-White, Great-Radiant. Brinton also gives this explanation (<u>The Myths of the New World</u>, 165. New York 1868); de Charencey obtained it from him.

16. De Charencey, op. cit. I: 10-12, after Nicolas Perrot: <u>Mémoire sur les moeurs, coutumes et religions de l'Amérique septentrionale</u>, publié par le R. P. Tailhau (Leipzig et Paris, 1864), ch. I: 3, 5. The other variants of this tale are from de Charencey, 20-21, 24-25.

17. Veselovskij, <u>Razyskanija</u> XX: 118-120.

2 Ancient Iran is devoid of stories of the creation of the world resembling the Slavic and the Turkic. — The continental character of the Iranian cosmogonies. — All that could possibly have passed from the Iranians to the Slavs and Turks are some general dualistic ideas and tales of the creation of the world. — The possibility of an Iranian embellishment upon an oceanic cosmogonic tale which took origin outside Iran. Examples of such tales in the Indian written and folk literature. — It is possible that some such tale passed from India into the domain of Iranian influence mediated by the Chaldeans: the oceanism in the Chaldeo-Semitic cosmogonies. — From the mingling of Iranian dualism with Chaldean oceanism has come the story found in the Slavic and Turkic dualistic tales of the world-creation. The enhanced significance of Ahriman in the Irano-Chaldean system of the Zervanites. — Elaboration of the Irano-Chaldean cosmogonic conceptions in the doctrines of the Gnostics and the Manicheans. — Anthropo-zoomorphic tales in the new religious doctrines of the III-VI centuries A. D.

We have seen that some investigators explained the Slavic dualistic legends of the world-creation from the influence of Iranian conceptions. This opinion has been expressed only on the basis of the fact that Iran is the classic region of religious dualism, and also because the Slavic Bogomilism, whose influence upon the ethnic legends is hard not to acknowledge, was genetically connected with the Armenian Paulicianism, and the latter with Iranian Manicheanism.

However, the sacred literature of pre-Islamic Iran affords us nothing like the plot in the Slavic or Turkic tales of the creation of the world by God and Satanail, even though it contains various dualistic ideas and images, which have passed into the oral literature even of some of the European peoples more westerly than the Slavs. Beside this, Iran is a continental country, especially northeastern Iran, where the base of the sacred Iranian literature was laid; and for this reason legends of an oceanic character could not have arisen there.

The Zend Avesta has been preserved in very incomplete form, and probably for this reason we do not find in it any single connected cosmogonic tale, but only fragmentary references to the creation of various objects, some by Ormuzd some by Ahriman.

The greater number of these references is contained in the first chapters of the parts of the Avesta preserved to this day, and known under the title Vendidad. Thus for instance in the first chapter of this book Ormuzd (properly Ahura-Mazda) enumerates those regions which he had created in obtaining the material world, and the opposites of those regions, which Ahriman (Angro-Mainyus) had created thereupon. Among these opposites we encounter as natural phenomena: winter and cold in general, hail, scorching heat, and also animals, both real and fabulous: the river-dragon, insects harmful to cattle, beast of prey and biting insects, and finally sins: false accounts, worship of false gods, burial of the dead in the earth, unbelief, cremation of the dead, etc.[1]

Beside this tale we meet in the Zend Avesta only fragmentary indications: in passing, Ormuzd is called the creator of the stars and the moon,[2] water and plants,[3] people,[4] dogs,[5] various beings which live on the earth and above it, in the water, in the air, etc.[6]

Along with the words of praise in which Ormuzd shines forth as the creator of the various divine and, to man, beneficent beings, the Zend Avesta describes Ahriman as the creator of the evil demons, the bringers of material and ethico-religious evils.[7]

In the later Iranian sacred book, the Bundahish (Creation), the editing of which happened as late as the Sassanid period, we encounter one tale of the creation of the world.

Although obviously it contains consequences of the influence of Chaldean oceanic tales, the cosmogony of the Bundahish has preserved in its base a continental character far more than is done for instance in the Biblical cosmogony. But along with this preservation of the ancient Iranian character, the cosmogony of the Bundahish has already altered in form the earlier Iranian dualism, by giving to Ahriman a more subordinate position. The evil deity creates independently as well as ruins (but only for a limited period) the creation of the good Ormuzd.

According to the Bundahish, Ormuzd and Ahriman existed separated from each other by a desert space, which some call the air.

Ormuzd, being omnisicient, knew that Ahriman exists, and that he devises only mischief; so he created invisible beings which might be useful to him. And they lived for 3000 years without material manifestation. Ahriman, being nescient, did not know of Ormuzd's existence; emerging out of the depths, he came into the world. When he beheld Ormuzd's world, he ran to kill its creator, out of desire to kill. But when he saw the bravery, the capacity for victory and the power of the spirits created by Ormuzd, he fled back into the darkness and created many demons (Daevas and Drujas), beings thirsty for the kill, and emerged to fight. When Ormuzd saw the creations of Ahriman, horrible, stinking, ugly, they seemed to him unworthy of praise; on the other hand, when Ahriman beheld the creations of Ormuzd, he found them worthy of praise, and he praised the creation of Ormuzd.

Although Ormuzd knew what would be the outcome of his activities, he nevertheless went to meet Ahriman, proposed to him that they make peace, and said to him: "Ahriman, give aid to my creations, give praise to them, and in reward your creations shall also be immortal, unalterable, without voice and without stench." Ahriman answered Ormuzd's proposals with a refusal and declared eternal war upon his creations. He did this because he thought that Ormuzd is powerless, and that only for this reason was he proposing peace. And the omniscient Ormuzd knew all: If I do not appoint a time when we shall fight, he may enslave my creatures and gain possession of them. Therefore Ormuzd said to Ahriman: "Appoint the time for the battle, let it be 9000 years." For he knew that after the time appointed, Ahriman would become powerless. Ahriman, who did not know the future, was content with this agreement. The omniscient Ormuzd knew that of these 9000 years, 3000 would pass according to his will, another 3000 under the mixed wills of Ormuzd and Ahriman, and in the final 3000 years Ahriman would be powerless and would be contained by Ormuzd's creatures. Then Ormuzd spoke a prayer (Ahuna vairya, etc.: "As the Lord said," etc.), which consists of twenty-one words, and showed Ahriman the end of his victory, Ahriman's impotence, the fall of the Demons, the resurrection (of the dead) and the future life, the end to every struggle against the good creation.

Ahriman, when he learned of his impotence and the destruction of the demons, was filled with remorse and fell back into the darkness. . . . During the time of Ahriman's remorse, Ormuzd created many creatures: first of all he created Vohu-Mano (a spirit), who should see to the spread of Ormuzd's creations. Ahriman created at the beginning Mitaokhta and then Akomano (a demon). Of the world-creations, Ormuzd created first the heavens, then Vohu-Mano, and, that things might go well, the light in the world. . . . After this he created some other sacred beings, and Ahriman created from the world-darkness some more demons.

"Ormuzd created of all the worldly creations first the heaven, then the water, then land, fourthly plants, fifthly animals, sixthly man."[8]

Such is the basic tale of the Bundahish, in which the monotheistic element now prevails over the dualistic. In the ensuing chapters is related in detail how there were created the heavenly and earthly objects, but somewhat in disharmony with the basic tale, since in them there is given to Ahriman a larger participation in the creation. As we have said above, this participation consists not only in independent creation, but in the ruining of Ormuzd's creations.

For 3000 years at a stretch Ahriman was smitten by Ormuzd creatures, among whom is man. Finally, incited by his demons, Ahriman determined upon active combat with the creations of Ormuzd, and for this purpose he created first of all, out of the body of a frog, a special man for the female demon Djakhi. Ahriman with his demons flew into the world and seized one-third of the heaven; but he quickly became frightened and fell onto the earth in the form of a snake. Then he approached the water and began to bore into the earth; he dug himself in, then he approached the plants, the ox and man (Gaya Maretan), and the fire. . . For half a day he obscured the world, as though it had been plunged into the darkness of night. He heaped upon the earth harmful, biting, and poisonous animals, scorpions, lizards, frogs, snakes, et al., he covered the plant growth . . . so that they died; after that he fell upon the man and the ox and slew them.

Finally he came to the fire and mixed it with vapor and darkness. The planets began to fight with the earth, and mixed in among the immovable stars, and all creation blackened. But Ormuzd expelled Ahriman and his demons, and all fell into the hell which was at the place where Ahriman had dug up the snake. . . . Thus did good and evil become intermingled in the world.

Farther on, the Bundahish relates in detail how this mingling came about, how the seas took shape after the deluge which happened when the shining Tistria (Sirius) fought against the demons, after Ahriman attacked the water; the sea water became salty, because it mixed with parts of the decomposed animals of Ahriman which Tistria drowned (ch. VII); how the mountains were formed, after Ahriman dug out the snake; the mountains grew for 18 years (ch. VIII).[9] The plants dried up under the influence of Ahriman, but one of Ormuzd's spirits washed them in the water of Tistria, and thus appeared 10,000 curative herbs against 10,000 diseases created by Ahriman. Afterwards there were formed from them 120,000 kinds of plants (ch. IX). Beside this, out of the ground which had been fructified by the member of the ox which Ahriman had killed, there grew 55 plants of bread-type and 12 curative plants. At this same time, from the seed of this primeval ox were formed the bull and the cow and after that 272 kinds of animals (ch. X), the buck-goat and sheep, the camel, the pig, etc. (ch. XIV). The people of today have proceeded from the pair which were formed on the branches of the tree Rheum ribes. This tree had grown from the seed which flowed out from the first man killed by Ahriman.

From the first, this pair acknowledged Ormuzd as creator, but later they thought that the world is the deed of Ahriman; and at the instigation of the devils they committed a whole series of sins: they ate fruits brought to them by the demons, they killed and ate animals, they cut the trees, they were carnal. From this pair came others, the progenitors of the various peoples (ch. XV. Cf. the beginning of ch. XXXI.).[10]

Such are the cosmogonic conceptions of the religious books of the Iranians. When we compare them with the Slavic cosmogonic legends, with the Finno-Uralic and the Turkic, which have been collected in large numbers in the researches of Veselovskij, we must come to the conclusion that they resemble the Iranian only in the general dualistic idea and to some extent

in the disposition of the tale of the creation of the angels and
the demons, the animals useful and those harmful to man. It
may be assumed without any special effort, that the latter kind
of legend (zoogonic and phytogonic) which we encounter from
Siberia to Britain (cf. among others, Veselovskij, Razyskanija
VIII: 328-332, 458-459, XI: 94-96) have been formed under
the influence of the Iranian conceptions; but of course to some
extent with the participation of local materials and reworkings.
However, with this the resemblances among the Iranian cosmogonic tales, and the Indo-European and Northern Asiatic,
cease. In the Iranian sacred books we find nothing resembling
the oceanic dualistic legend of God and Satan which is recorded
with such minor differences in various regions of Eastern Europe and Northern Asia, from Bulgaria to the Yakut district.

We have already observed that the unusual similarity
among the variants of this legend, from the Bulgarian to the
Yakut, forces us to assume that all these variants must have
come from one common source and that they spread under the
action of some strong cultural influence. This source must be
sought for in Asia, since the particularly wide development of
the legend that concerns us among the Siberian Turks excludes
every assumption that it could have spread there under the influence of the Christian apocryphal legends that were brought
to Siberia with the Russian colonization; which is comparatively
recent and still is weak in the district of the Upper Irtysh and
the Lena.

Except for the Japanese tales indicated by Charencey (which
are very far from the Slavic and the Turkic), or other Asiatic
cosmogonic legends (in which the earth is extracted from the
water) only a few are known to us: the Indian. The simplest
probably, and probably also the oldest form of these tales we
find in the Satapatha Brahmana (XIV, 1. ch. 11): "In the beginning the earth was as broad as the palm of a hand. A boar
named Emush drew it out. Its master, Prajapati gave him for
this a female companion."

According to other Indian books, this boar is the incarnation of Prajapati-Brahma himself.

In the Taittirya Sanhita (VII, 1.5.1 et seq.) Prajapati first
becomes a wind and stirs up the primeval ocean; he sees the
earth in the depths of the ocean; he turns himself into a boar
and draws the earth up. The Taittirya Brahmana relates: "This

[the universe] was first water, flux. Prajapati asked himself:
'How may this develop?' He observed a lotus leaf which floated
on the water and thought, 'There must be something on which
this rests.' In the form of a boar he plunged into the water near
the lotus leaf. He found earth down below. After breaking off
a piece of it, he returned to the surface of the water and placed
it on the lotus leaf. As far as he spread it, so large is the expanse of this broad object."[11]

This theme is elaborated with details in the Puranas, where
the boar appears either directly as the incarnation of Brahma,
or as Vishnu who emanated from him.[12]

The tale of Vishnu-Brahma is interesting to us because we
find in it one more detail of the Slavic and Turkic cosmogonic
tales; namely, that the divine boar, after it had extracted the
earth from the water, built a mountain on it.

According to the opinion of Lyall (Études sur les moeurs
religieuses et morales de l'extrême orient, French transl.,
p. 80), the conception of the divine boar the Indian Aryans took
over from the ancient population of the peninsula; so that the
whole base of the story of extracting the earth by the boar must
be ascribed to this non-Aryan population. In any case, this
story is set forth in the Indian sacred books in the thought-
guise of the later unitarian, pantheistic-messianic world-view
of the Brahmins. Only in the Satapatha Brahmana do we see
that the boar is separate from the supreme deity, and this
recalls the dualism of the Slavic tales and those like them. In
the Puranas, God in the form of the boar draws forth out of
the ocean the entire earth: this must be considered as a sub-
sequent reworking of the theme.

In the Satapatha Brahmana and the Taittirya Brahmana
there have been preserved a few details which must be considered to be older: according to the first, when the earth was
drawn forth from the ocean it was as large only as the palm of
a hand; according to the second, only some particles of the
earth were wrested from the depth, and afterwards the creator
expanded these particles.

All these three details show that the Indian tales are of a
kind with the Slavic and the Turkic, and they permit the assumption that there is genetic connection between them. Since the
Indian tales are written down in an oceanic region, while the
Slavic and Turkic are from a continental region, the former

must be considered to be the original, while the latter have
been borrowed from them.

In any case, this borrowing never could have been immediate. The Indian tales lack what is most essential in the Slavic
and the Turkic: the antagonism between the two creators. Some
analogies to this antagonism are visible in the cosmogonic tale
of the Taittirya Arenyaka (I, 23), where it is told how at first
everything was water, how Prajapati was born on the lotus, and
how the tortoise was formed from the water that was on his
body. The latter immediately began to quarrel with Prajapati,
who said: "You have proceeded from my skin and my flesh."
"No," replied the turtle, "I was here first," etc.[13]

In the present Hindu oral literature a tale has been taken
down, in which we encounter a trait which occurs also in the
plot of the tales that concern us; namely, the diving of God
into the depths of the sea and the antagonism of the gods. This
tale, evidently, belongs to that cycle of legends which relates
the incarnation of Vishnu in the form of a boar. According to
this tale, once Brahma, who found himself upon a lotus in the
midst of the ocean, seeing nothing else in the world, believed
himself to be the first of all creations. He descended the stem
of the lotus and met Naroyana (Vishnu), who was sleeping.
Brahma asked him: "Who art thou?" "I am the first-born!"
answered Vishnu. Brahma began to quarrel, and even attacked
Vishnu. But as they fought, Mahadeva (Siva) threw himself in
to separate them and said: "I am the first-born; but I will
recognise as the older him who will be in position to see the
crown of my head and the sole of my foot!"

Vishnu incarnated himself as a boar, dug into the earth
and came forth into the lower regions, where he saw the foot
of Mahadeva, who acknowledged Vishnu, after he resumed form,
as the oldest among the gods. (Burnouf: L'Inde Française,
and De Gubernatis: Mythologie Zoologique II: 89, note.)

There are here some analogies with the Slavic tales, and
likewise with the Yezid, the trans-Caucasian, and the gypsy,
which we shall present later.

But all these similarities between the above-cited Indian
tales and the Slavic and Turkic cosmogonic legends are not
adequate for placing these latter in direct genetic connection
with the former; in fact such a connection is impossible, since
the given tribes are not geographic neighbors.

The Slavic and Turkic tales could have proceeded straight from the Indian only under one condition: namely, if the Indian legends had been appropriated by the intermediary peoples and if these legends had been reworked in such a way that they should approach more nearly those which we find now from Bulgaria to the Yakut region.

In that intermediary region, the Indian theme would have had to take on a dualistic tinge.

Such a reworking would have had to take place under the influence of the Iranian cosmogonic conceptions which we have expounded above.

However, between the actual Iranian cosmogonies and the Indian the difference is so great (this corresponds, among other things, also to the respective geographic conditions of Iran and Hindustan) that it would have been quite impossible for the Iranians simply to appropriate directly the above-cited Indian tale. The assimilation of the various cosmogonic conceptions would have had to take place in a region favorable to it, such as Chaldea, which has had its own oceanic cosmogonies and its dualism; while at the same time, in consequence of its ancient relations and its having belonged to the Persian kingdom of the Achaemenids and later of the Parthians and the Sassanids, Chaldea has been subjected to Iranian influence and on its side has influenced the Iranians and the peoples subject to them. Chaldea or Babylonia is a coastland country. Its population already 3000-4000 years before Christ had relations by sea with the various countries — at least as far as the Sinai Peninsula — so that it knew well the Indian Ocean also.[14]

Moreover, this country of deltas, subject to the overflows of such large rivers as the Euphrates and Tigris, is at the same time a country of canals. For all these reasons the cult of water and of what pertains to water are completely natural matters in Chaldea. The fish-like god Ea (Oannes of Berosus) appears in Chaldea as a demiurge and educator. Especially in the city of Babylon did the personality of this water god and fish become fused with the personality of Bel-Merodach, and in Assyria with Bel-Ashur, at the base of whom one must seek for some solar deity. According to the fragments of Babylono-Assyrian cosmogonies, which have been preserved in unfortunately badly broken tablets with cuneiform Assyrian inscriptions, there existed at first the boundless abyss (Apsu) and the chaotic sea (Mummu Tiamat), and out of them came later the gods and the creators. In one of these inscriptions Assur creates the earth above the sea and the dry land on the sea.[15]

Such a cosmogony entered into the base of the cosmogonic conceptions of all the myth-making peoples — the Phoenicians[16] and even the Hebrews with their primeval darkness that was above the abyss, and with the wind (roah' — at first wind, later on the spirit of God) which moved over the water. In this cosmogony there are dualistic elements, in the sense that there are presented real cosmic beginnings and divine persons, the latter of which appear and act two by two. But a dualism in the sense of a struggle still is lacking here. However, since similar dualism exists more or less in all mythologies and religions, it could not but have entered into the cosmogonies of the Chaldeans.

According to one of the Assyrian inscriptions, between Merodach and Tiamat there was immediate war. This struggle is represented here in anthropomorphic imagery,[17] while in the celebrated fragment from Berosus it says that the primeval chaotic beings, which were composed of mixed parts (a bull with a human head, etc.), were created by a woman Tavat (Tiamat), i.e., the sea, and that long afterwards Bel (Bel-Merodach) set the world in order; beginning by splitting this woman into two parts and making from the one half the heaven, and from the other the earth.[18]

Tales such as these obviously contain dualism, and that of a nature that ascribes the creation of the world to the moist beginning, identified with darkness, and not with the wind and light. We already see here the basis of that dualism which in the first centuries of Christianity was set forth by the Gnostics and which exerted a strong influence upon the formation of the dualistic legends of the various Asiatic and European peoples. This Chaldean basis of dualism with an oceanic environment in the cosmogony must have been a very congenial medium for the reception of foreign cosmogonic tales, such as the Indian oceanic and the Iranian dualistic ones. The Indian oceanic tales, like those adduced above, in which is told how God extracted particles of the earth out of the sea, could have passed from Hindustan to Chaldea as easily as the Chaldean tale of the deluge did pass into the Indian sacred writings. As for the borrowing activity of the Chaldean and Iranian religious conceptions, it is something long demonstrated. The Iranians took from the Chaldeans the goddess Anaiti, and the Chaldeans reinforced the germs of their dualism with Iranian conceptions.

The Greeks and even a part of the Iranians identified the Iranian Magi with the Chaldeo-Babylonian priests. In the Greco-Babylonian literature, Zoroaster even was placed among the ancient Chaldean kings. The Chaldean conceptions helped to soften the sharpness of the Iranian dualism, by contributing to the elaboration of the conceptions of the primeval principle, endless time (Zrvan Akaran), from which principle there proceeded Ormuzd and Ahriman.[19] Beside this, although the ancient conceptions of the predominance of Ormuzd were strengthened by idealism, none the less the significance of Ahriman as the representative of matter, was elevated even more, instead of sinking.

According to some Zervanitic tales, which have come down to us through the Armenians and some Islamic writers, Ahriman was born before Ormuzd.[20] From this it is no great distance to the ideas which lay at the base of the tales and which were diffused in the time of the Sassanids even among the Orthodox Iranians; according to which tales Ormuzd created the light (sun, moon) at the counsel of Ahriman;[21] it is not far from the tale which got into the Bundahish, namely, that Ahriman created man; even though the Bundahish does not dwell upon this, and represents man as actually the creation of the she-demon Djakhi, distinct from the human type created by Ormuzd.

A similar reworking of the ancient Iranian dualism upon the base of the Chaldean oceanic conceptions, with an enhanced significance to what, according to the ancient Iranian conceptions, was only an evil foe of the good creator — such a reworking, it can be seen, constituted the peculiarity of the Chaldean cosmogonic ideas in the epoch when the Christian sects appeared.

The author of the notable essay Philosophoumena, who gives us many data on the beliefs of the various religious communities in Hither Asia of the III century A.D., tells us this about the cosmogonies of the Chaldeans which the author ascribes to Zoroaster (Zaratas):

"The basic causes of all beings are two: the Father and the Mother. The Father is the light, the

Mother is the darkness. The parts of the light are
heat, dryness, lightness, speed; the parts of the
darkness are cold, dampness, heaviness, sloth. The
world is composed of all these, out of the combination
of the two principles: the male and the female; and
as for the origin of the things which we find upon the
earth and in the whole world, here is what Zaratas
says: There are two deities, one heavenly and the
other earthly. To the earthly deity belongs the derivation of everything which the earth generates; that
is, water. The heavenly deity is fire, which has the
attributes of the air, and at one and the same time is
cold and heat . . ."[22]

The Gnostics developed these already quite syncretistic
conceptions and still further shifted the construction of the various cosmogonies, from the Iranian to the Egyptian; yet holding themselves primarily to the bases of the Semitic cosmogonies.

The Gnostics had two tasks. The one was philosophical:
to explain the dualism of matter and spirit; the other, historico-
religious: to reconcile especially the Hebrew conceptions as
they are set forth in the Bible, with the ideas of the universal
syncretic theosophy, which was elaborated in the minds of
various individuals in the Alexandrian and Roman epoch through
the meeting of the various religions of the ancient world and
Greek philosophy. To this second task there was added a third:
to explain the discrepancies between all the Testamental conceptions of God and the ideas about Christ, whose individuality
in the conceptions of the Christians of the II-III centuries fused
with the ideas concerning the universal mind — the Word
(λόγος) of the Alexandrian and Asia Minor Platonists.

All thse problems the Gnostics tried to solve, by declaring
spirit (idea, mind, light) and matter (darkness, etc.) as entities,
and the present world as the product of their conflict and inter-
mingling. The Hebrew national and Old Testament God, according to the Gnostics, is distinct from the universal god who
had revealed himself in the person of Jesus Christ, and assumes
the role of creator of the material world; in this respect he is
identified with the antagonist of Christ: Satan.[23]

Harnack presents very vividly the struggle toward a universal
religion, which appears, after the attempts of the Gnostics, in
Neo-Platonism, Catholicism, and Manicheanism. All these,
although they have a common base in many respects, differ in

the following: Neo-Platonism holds more to the beginning of the natural polytheistic religions in a spirit of pantheism; Catholicism rests upon the Hebrew religious traditions which had taken on in their later development the character of monotheism; and Manicheanism proceeds from the Iranian dualism with its Syro-Chaldean admixtures.[24]

Toward the middle of the IV century, Catholicism already prevails over Neo-Platonism; but then its struggle with Manicheanism begins; which struggle (if one keeps in mind the spread of Manicheanism in the form of Armenian Paulicianism, Greco-Slavic Catharism and Bogomilism with its western offshoots, Albigensianism, etc.) continues almost to the end of the Middle Ages.

The Iranian Mani or Manas developed in the III century A.D. a syncretistic Irano-Chaldean dualism in a strictly logical theocosmosophy with a corresponding ascetic ethic.[25] According to the teaching of Mani, God, i.e. Light, and the "region of darkness" are eternal.

From the latter proceeded Satan, and he began to attack the light. Then the light god created, along with his <u>Syzygy,</u> "the spirit of his justice," the first man, who undertook the struggle with the devil. But Satan defeated the man and seized from him some particles of the light. By mixing these particles with elements of the darkness, the Devil created the visible world and in it actual man — Adam. The primeval man appeared in the form of the non-suffering Christ (Jesus impatibilis), and preached to the people the truth at the time when the Jesus created by Satan was preaching the lie.

So it is that we find in Manicheanism materials such as we find in the Slavic legends and in the apocryphas of the creation of the world by Satanail, and so also the antagonism between Christ and the ruler of the world before him; even though, of course, these materials are disposed in one way among the Manicheans and another in the Slavic tales.

Manicheanism spread far. Mani himself preached his doctrine in Iran, in Turkestan and western China (Chinese Turkestan), where Manicheanism was recognized as the official religion by a Turkic tribe as late as the X century A.D.

The followers of Mani carried his doctrine to the west to the Carthaginian region including Spain. The Manicheans wished to gain the masses of the people and so they preached by use

of tales and imagery. The circumstance is very important for
the history of the folk tales that Manicheanism appeared and
grew in an epoch when all the religious systems of Hither Aisa
in general were entering upon a period of imagery and anthro-
pomorphism, in consequence of the fact that these religious
systems were emerging from the narrower priestly-philosophica
circles and were beginning to spread among the common people.
It was precisely in this time that in Christianity there were
formed the anthropomorphic legends about the Holy Trinity and
the Virgin Mary, the symbolizations of the Holy Ghost and of
the apostles in the shape of animals. In this same time, in the
Chaldeo-Iranian world, along with the official and literary
Avestanism, Zervanism, etc. there spread, e.g., legends about
Ormuzd and Ahriman: how they were born, how the latter con-
versed with Zervan and taught Ormuzd to create all bodies, how
the two gods dined together with their children, etc.[26]

Similar tales traveled along with the Manichean teachings
and created a whole cycle of legends, which bear to the doctrine
of Mani the same relationship as the Catholic legends, especially the apocryphal ones, bear to the teachings of the gospels.

Among these legends — we may say, among these Manichean apocryphas, there must have occurred the bases of the
dualistic tales of the world-creation, which are our concern
here, and which must have taken shape in the Irano-Chaldean
country in the manner described above. We now find reflections
of these legends precisely where either directly or indirectly
the Manichean preaching penetrated.

Notes

1. Vendidad, Fargard I; Avesta, trad. par C. de Harlez;
7-12.

2. Yaçna I: XI — 34.

3. Yaçna IV: XXI — 48.

4. Vispered XIII: 11.

5. Vendidad XIII: 6

6. Khorda Avesta, Yasht XV.

7. Yaçna IX: 8, Vendidad III: XXII: 72-74; etc. etc.

8. Der Bundehesch, übers. von Justi, Ch. I: 1 — 3.

9. According to the authors of the Bundahish, the earth normally should be flat and smooth; it will be thus again after the final defeat of Ahriman. (Cf. Bundahish, Justi's transl. Ch. XXXI).

10. It seems to us that Ch. XV is a not perfectly smooth composition of 2 variants. Certain of its contradictions with the details of the Zend-Avesta and certain of its agreements with the traditions of the Semites (among the Phoenicians it is Eok — Havath — Eve who brings herself to eat the fruits) lead us to suppose that the material of this chapter derives from Babylonian traditions. At all events it is impossible not to notice in this tale the spiritual and therefore later priestly-philosophical conceptions of the sin-and-fall of the first people; the sin inheres in the food, the killing of living creatures, and in sexual union. (Cf. Ch. XXX — prior to the advent of the Messiah Saoshyant people ceased to eat meat, then fruits and milk, yet later they ceased to drink water and eventually they got along completely without food.) Since we find fragments of this tale also among peoples less advanced than the Babylonians, this favors the supposition that these peoples borrowed the details of the tales directly or indirectly from the Babylonians.
    Among the Hebrews the episode of the first sin (eating the fruit) has taken on the character of a moral fable (punishment for disobedience) and has intermixed some features of the tale of the god who was jealous of men (a sort of Promethean myth). Further along we shall encounter reverberations of the conception that lay at the basis of Ch. XV of the Bundahish, among the tales of the tribes of the Altai.

11. All three tales in Muir: Original Sanskrit Texts, 2nd ed. I: 52-53.

12. Muir, op.cit. 50-51; Wilson: Vishnu Purana I, Ch. IV. Le Bhagavata Purana, trad. p. Eug. Burnouf, 1. I ch. 3, 1. III ch. 13.

13. Muir, Original Sanskrit Texts I: 32-38. The tortoise, as is known, appears as the support of the earth in many Indian cosmographies, and also as the incarnation of the deity in many Indian religious tales.

14. The ancient connections of Chaldea with the Sinai peninsula are indicated by the inscription on a statue found at

Tel-Lokh and chiseled in a kind of stone found about Sinai. The illustrious Assyriologist Sayce has unearthed in India also a muslin which the Babylonians called <u>Sindhu</u> (Hebr. <u>sadin</u>, Grk. σινδών). A. H. Sayce: <u>Lectures on the Origin and Growth of Religion as Illustrated by the Religion of the Ancient Babylonians</u> 2nd ed., 138).

15. Lenormant: <u>Les origines de l'histoire d'après le Bible et les traditions des peuples orientaux.</u> 2° ed. I: 496-497.

16. Lenormant, op. cit. 507 seq.

17. We have seen the primeval nature of the wind in the Indian cosmogony, where God, after his appearance as a wind, turns himself into a boar. Among the Hebrews, God and the wind take on the form of a bird: Wünsche: <u>Der Midrasch — Bereschit Bara</u>, 10. As in other cosmogonies (among this number are also some Indian), there appears as the primeval creator a divine bird, which lays a cosmic egg on the sea. This egg, however, is not found in the Hebrew conceptions, which have been expurgated by the rabbis. In the further development of the Hebrew religious conceptions, the bird-demiurge is transformed into a dove, a favorite of Semitic traditions from the Tigris to the Mediterranean Sea. For the development of the Hebrew conceptions of roah' out of the wind to the spirit of God (roah' Elohim), cf. the article of Sabatier: <u>Notion hébraïque de l'Esprit</u>, in the Essays of La faculté de théologie protestante de Paris presented to M. Edouard Reuss. Paris 1879, p. 5f.

18. Lenormant, op. cit. 506-507.

19. James Darmsteter: <u>Ormazd et Ahriman, leurs origines, leur histoire</u> (Bibliothèque de l'école des hautes études; Sciences philologiques et historiques XXIX: 314 seq.)

20. Darmsteter, op. cit. 324-325. "Uléma i Islam" states that Zervan created first of all fire and water, and from their mingling was born Ormuzd, who descried Ahriman in the depth of the abyss. The Armenian scribes (Eznikh and Elisée) have preserved for us an official manifesto from the Sassanid epoch (V century A.D.) in which it is said that Ahriman appeared in the world earlier than Ormuzd (Darmsteter, op. cit. 324-327). Elisée Vartabad: <u>Soulèvement national de l'Arménie chrétienne au V-e siècle contre la loi de Zoroastre</u> (Paris 1844). 26-27, 311-318.

21. According to Eznikh's note to the French translation of Elisée; p. 313.

22. "Philosophoumena", ed. Miller, I, z. Lenormant, op. cit. 530. In another place the author of the "Philosophoumena" calls Zoroaster the teacher of Pythagoras, the male principle the monad, the female (the earth) the diad, etc.

23. For the Gnostics, consult Matter's essay, Histoire critique du gnosticisme (1828; which retains its significance despite its age); but further, Hilgenfeld: Die Ketzergeschichte des Urchristentums (1884) in Koffmann: Die Gnosis nach ihrer Tendenz und Organisation. For the general character of Gnosticism and its appraisal with respect to the development of Christianity from apostolic to ecclesiastical or Catholic, consult Harnack: Lehrbuch der Dogmengeschichte, 2nd. ed. I (1888).

24. Harnack, op. cit. 731-738.

25. Of the latest essay particularly on Manicheanism by Kessler (Mani, I: 1888), only the first part has appeared so far; it is devoted to analysis of sources. For the present Kessler sets forth his views in his article Mani und Manichäer in Herzog's Realencyclopädie für protestantische Theologie, 2nd ed.; in which he emphasizes the presence of Chaldean elements in Manicheanism. The article is summarized by Chantepie de la Soussay in Lehrbuch der Religiongeschichte; also by Harnack in Lehrbuch der Dogmengeschichte. To date the fullest account of Manicheanism is supplied by Flügel's Mani, seine Lehre und seine Schriften, 1862, and by Spiegel: Eranische Altertumskunde, vol. II.

26. Elisée Vartabad, op. cit. 313.

3 Reflexes of the Irano-Chaldean cosmogonic tales in the area of the Altaian Turks and Mongols. — Remnants of these tales in Mesopotamia, Armenia, and Trans-Caucasia: the cosmogonic concepts of the Mandeans (Sabeans) and Yezids; the Grusian legends. — Traits common to the Yezid and the Ukrainian traditions that have become particularized in the Christmas carols of the three doves. — The legends of the creation of the world among the Magyar gypsies; remnants of Irano-Chaldean conceptions in them. — Addendum: the delineation of the world-tree and the gods associated with it in the Assyro-Babylonian and the Yezid monuments.

In the northeastern corner of the region where Manicheanism spread, we now find cosmogonic tales with dualistic character which must be considered to be the nearest likenesses of the Chaldeo-Iranian legends we have assumed — the direct source of the similar legends in the folk literature of eastern Europe and northern Asia.

We mean here the tales of the Altaian Turks and their neighbors, the Mongolians.

Most characteristic is the tale printed in Radloff, <u>Proben der Volkslitteratur der türkischen Stämme Südsibiriens</u>, I: 175-184. Here are the most important parts of this tale:[1]

Before the earth was completed, all was water, there was no earth, there was no sky, there were no sun and moon. God flew about, yet another man flew about, both flew about being black geese. God was thinking about nothing at all; that man, by stirring up the wind, disturbed the water and splashed water in God's face. That man thought to raise himself higher than God; instead, he plunged downward and fell into the water. Having plunged down he spoke, almost strangled: "Oh my God, save me." God spoke: "O man, raise yourself up from out of the water." Now that man arose from out of the water on high. God spoke: "Let there be a firm rock." From the floor of the sea there came forth a hard rock; the man sat down on its face, and he lived together with God.

God spoke: "Do thou descend to the floor of the sea and bring up earth." After he had descended, he seized some earth with his hand, and when he had brought the earth, he gave it to God. God cast this earth over the surface of the sea and spoke: "Let there be land." Thereupon there was land. Then God spoke again: "Descend and bring up yet more earth." The man thought to himself: "If I go down there, I will bring earth for myself also." He descended to the depth of the water, and took two handfuls according to his thought. The one handful he brought to God, with the other he put the earth in his mouth and rose up, so as to make land himself, hidden from God. The one handful of earth he gave to God; God took it, scattered it about, and the earth became thick. That man put the earth in his mouth, it swelled up, the man started to choke, it stopped his throat and he was almost at the point of dying. Now he ran away; but when he looked around, God stood at his side. As that man was close to strangling, he spoke to God: "O God, very God, save me!" God spoke: "What wert thou up to? Didst thou think perhaps that thou couldst take earth and hide it in thy mouth? Why didst thou hide the earth?" That man spoke: "I put earth in my mouth to make land." God said: "Spit it out!" When the man had spat it out, there came to be the little swamp-hillocks. Thereupon God spoke: "Now art thou in sin. Thou thoughtst to do me ill; the inner mind of the people who are subject to thee will be evil likewise. The mind of the people who are subject to me shall be holy. They shall see the sun, they shall see the light, I shall be called the true Kurbystan. Thy name shall be Erlik. The man who shall hide his sin from me shall be thine, a man of Erlik. The man who shall hide himself from thy sin shall be mine!"

There grew up a single tree without limbs. God noticed it.[2] "A single tree without limbs is not pleasant to see; let nine limbs come to be on it," he said. Nine limbs grew out. "At the bases of the nine limbs let there be nine humans, from those nine humans let nine peoples arise."

When thereupon Erlik came, there sounded a noise from many things (that were unknown to him). Now Erlik said to God: "Whence cometh this noise?" God said: "Thou art a prince, I too am a prince, this is my people." Then said Erlik: "Oh give me this people of thine." God said, "No, I will not give them to thee; wait thou." Now Erlik said to himself: "Hold, hold, I must look over this people of God's." Erlik went and went, he came there. As he looked, he saw everything — humans, wild animals, birds, all sorts of living things. Erlik said: "How did God make all this? I said I was going to take everything, how shall this be done, on what does this people feed itself?"

When Erlik saw that they ate from one side of the single tree, but not from the other, he said: "Why do you eat only from this?"

Then spoke one of the humans: "This is our food which God showed unto us. God has said to mankind: 'Do not eat the food of these four limbs; toward the sunrise there are five limbs, eat the food from these!' After he had so spoken, he ascended into heaven; at the foot of the tree he has set a dog, saying: 'If the devil comes, seize him.' Moreover, he has set a snake, saying, 'If the devil comes, bite him.' Thereupon God spoke to the dog and to the snake, saying: 'If a man comes to eat from the food of the five limbs which lie to the sunrise, let him approach; but if he wishes to eat of these four limbs, do not let him near!' Therefore this is our food."

When the devil Erlik heard this, he went to the tree; there he found a human by the name of Töröngöi; to him he spoke: "If God hath told thee thou mightest eat from these five limbs, and not to eat from those four, then is this a lie and not the truth. Do not eat the food from these five limbs; eat it from those four limbs."

When the devil had so spoken, the snake fell asleep. The devil entered into the snake; inside the snake the devil spoke: "Climb up into this tree." The snake climbed up into the tree. The snake ate of the food which God had told mankind they should not eat. There lived at this time with the man Töröngöi a girl by the name of Edji; to these the snake said: "Töröngöi, Edji, eat this!" Töröngöi said; "No, how should I eat, God himself hath said, 'Do not eat.' I will not eat." Thereupon the snake gave to the girl the food; Edji ate it. As she ate it, the food was very sweet. Töröngöi did not eat. Thereupon Edji stripped off the fruit and touched it to Töröngöi's mouth. Then the hair fell from their bodies and they were ashamed. One hid behind one tree, the other hid behind another tree.

Then God came. When God came, all the people hid from God. God called, "Töröngöi, Töröngöi, Edji, Edji, where are you?" When God called, they said: "We are on trees, and we will not come to thee." God said: "What is the matter with thee, Töröngöi?"

"Edji touched my mouth with the food that thou didst forbid." God said: "Why hast thou done this, Edji?" Edji said: "The snake said to me, 'Eat!'" God said: "Snake! What was the matter with thee?" It said: "A devil had entered inside me, I did not say it, but the devil said it." God said: "How did the devil enter into thee?" The snake said: "I had fallen asleep, then the devil came to me." God said: "Dog, what was the matter with thee? Why didst thou not seize the devil?" The dog said; "To my eyes he was invisible."

Now God spoke to the snake: "O snake! Now hast thou become the devil, may man become thine enemy, and beat thee and kill thee." Then he spoke to Edji: "Thou hast eaten the bread which I told thee not to eat, thou hast given ear to the word of the devil, thou hast eaten of the devil's food; now shalt thou bear children, thou shalt experience great pain, death shall overtake thee." Then said God to Töröngöi: "Thou hast eaten of the devil's food, thou hast not harkened to my word, thou hast harkened to the devil's words; whoever follows after the devil's words is in the devil's land; he who does not harken to my words will not see my light, he will not receive my mercy, and he will remain in darkness. Now is the devil an enemy to me; and along with the devil art thou, Töröngöi, likewise my enemy. Hadst thou not eaten the devil's food, hadst thou received my blessing, hadst thou followed my words, thou wouldst have become like unto me; now may nine sons and nine daughters be born to thee. Now hast thou received the devil's blessing, thou hast eaten the devil's food. I will no more create humans, now let man arise out of himself."

Now God spoke to the devil: "Why hast thou deceived my man?" Erlik spoke: "When I asked thee, thou didst not give them, I have stolen them, I have taken them with cunning; when they ride off on horses, I will cast them down; when they drink brandy I will cause them to fall out among themselves, I will make them fight and beat each other with boughs. When they go down to the water, I will cause them to fall down, when they climb upon rocks, I will push them off."

Now God said: "Beneath three earth-layers is the land of darkness, where there is neither sun nor moon; there I will cast thee down. Now I will give food no more myself, you shall feed yourselves of your own power; I will come no more to converse with you, I will send you Mai-Terè, he shall teach you to make all sorts of things."

Mai-Terè came to them, taught them all things;
what Mai-Terè prepared for them was barley, radishes,
kandyk, lily-bulbs, and onions. Then said the devil:
"Now, Mai-Terè, plead to God for me, I would fain
raise myself up to God's side." Mai-Terè bowed before
God for sixty-two years. God spoke: "Yes, if thou
wilt not provoke enmity with me, if thou wilt do mankind no evil, then come!" Now Erlik rose up to heaven;
when Erlik had come thither, he bowed before God:
"Give me thy blessing, give me thy blessing, that I
may perfect the heaven, O God!" God gave him the
blessing: "Perfect thou the heaven," said he. Now
Erlik with God's blessing made the heaven, and Erlik's
devils grew in his heaven, they grew great in number.

There lived also a man of God Mandi-Shirè, who
thought to himself: "Our mankind live upon the earth,
Erlik's mankind live in heaven, this is indeed very
bad." Thus thought Mandi-Shirè, he became provoked
with God, and he went to war with Erlik. Erlik came
against Mandi-Shirè, smote Mandi-Shirè with fire,
and drove him away. Mandi-Shirè fled homeward. God
asked him: "Whence comest thou?" Mandi-Shirè spoke
to God: "Erlik's people live above in heaven, our people live on earth, this is very bad. I bethought myself
to cast Erlik's people down to earth, but I had not the
power and I could not cast them down." God spoke:
"No one is stronger than I, Erlik now is stronger than
thou; his time is not yet come; when his time comes,
then shall I say to thee: 'Today go'; if thou goest on
that day, thou shalt be the stronger."

He lived, he lived quietly; when Mandi-Shirè had
so lived for long, he thought to himself: "The day on
which God saith 'Today go' is come." God saw Mandi-
Shirè and said: "Thou shalt drive him forth, thou shalt
carry out thy thought, thou shalt be strong, very strong
shalt thou be; my mighty blessing shall come upon thee."
Mandi-Shirè rejoiced, he laughed, laughed, and he
spoke: "I have no gun, I have no quiver, no spear, and
no sword. Only one red hand have I, how shall I go?"
God spoke: "With what wouldst thou go?" Mandi-Shirè
said: "I have nothing; my foot will I place upon him,
with my arm I will cast him away." God said: "Take
this, take a spear." Mandi-Shirè took the spear, he
went to heaven, he conquered Erlik and drove him out.
Erlik's heaven he shattered with the spear, all that he
found therein he cast down. Before this time there was
no stone, no rock, no mountain forest. When now the
ruins of Erlik's heaven fell to earth, there came into
being all rocks, all stones, the mountain forest, the

high mountains and all mountain ridges; that land which
had been created by God, good, quite flat, became all
bad.   Thereupon Mandi-Shirè cast Erlik's subjects from
heaven down upon the earth.   Some fell into the water
and died, some fell upon the cattle and died, some fell
upon upright trees and died, some collided with humans
who were walking, some fell upon stones and died;
all died.

Now Erlik asked land of God.   "My heaven thou
hast broken, now I have no land, give me a little," he
said.   God said: "No, I will give thee no land.   Said
Erlik: "Give me but one acre of land."   God said; "No,
I will give thee no land whatever."   Erlik said: "Give
me five arm's-breadths of land."   God gave him not
even five arm's-breadths.   Now Erlik struck the stick
which he held in his hand, into the earth, and said:
"Oh my God, give me but as much land as the point
of this stick covers."   God laughed and said, "As much
land as lies under the point of this stick, do thou take."

Now Erlik began to build a heaven on this small
piece of land.   But God spoke: "Get thee below; build
it under the earth; there establish thou thyself.   Descend to the floor of hell, encompass thyself with
layers.   Above let there burn an unquenchable fire;
never, nevermore shalt thou again see the light of
sun or moon.   Sometime, at the end of the world, I
will judge thee; if thou comport thyself well, I will
lead thee into my light; if thou be evil, I will remove
thee once again as far; thus shall it be."   Erlik spoke:
"I have no subjects; now I have descended into the earth,
what can I do alone by myself?"   God spoke: "Why askest
thou me, do as thou thinkest to do, create thou thine
own mankind."   Then the devil bowed before God: "If
thou wilt bestow thy blessing, I will indeed create."
God gave the blessing.   Erlik made a bellows and laid
down a tong and struck it once with a hammer; from
under the hammer a frog jumped forth; again he struck
once, a snake wriggled forth; again he struck, there
came forth a bear and ran away; again he struck, there
came forth a wild pig; again he struck, there came
forth an almys (an evil, hairy spirit); again he struck,
there came forth a Shulumys (an evil spirit); again he
struck, there came forth a camel.

Now God came and cast Erlik's bellows, tong and
hammer into the fire; from the bellows cast into the
fire there arose a woman, from the tong and the hammer
there arose a man.   God took the woman, spat upon
her and she became a bird, she became a heron (kordoi),
from whose wings one does not feather an arrow, whose

flesh a dog will not eat, who makes the swamp to
stink. God spat upon the man, and he became a rat
(yalban), whose feet are long, who has no hands, who
is the filth of the house, who eats the soles of old
boots.

Then God spoke to mankind: "I have made for you
cattle, I have made for you food, I have caused lovely,
pure water to flow upon the surface of the earth that
you may drink it; I have helped you, now do ye good
also! Now will I go away, I will not return soon. Thou
art of my mankind, Shal-Jimè! A man who has drunk
brandy, small children, colts, calves, lambs, these
do thou protect, Shal-Jimè! The man who has died
well, him do thou take! Whoever has shot himself
with a gun, who has killed himself, him do not take,
cast him away. Whoever has died in combat with others,
him bring thou into my land. The man who has pur-
loined something from the rich, the one who has made
himself an enemy to others, him do not take, cast him
away; whoever has died for my sake, for the sake of
the prince, him bring thou into my land. I have helped,
I have removed the devil, I have separated him from
you; if the devil now approaches you, give the devil
food, but the devil's food do ye not eat. If you eat
the devil's food, you shall be the devil's subjects;
do not forget my words! When you call upon me, then
shall you sit upon my coat-tail. I will now remain
away; though I remain away a long time, yet will I
come again; never forget me, do not forget that I
will come. Think that I am really coming. Now I go
afar, when I return I will at that time see your good
and your evil. In my place now there shall help you
Yapkara, Mandi-Shirè, Shal-Jimè. Yapkara, see
well to it! If Erlik would take the dead of mankind,
tell it to Mandi-Shirè; Mandi-Shirè is strong, he will
conquer Erlik. Shal-Jimè, see well to it that the
evil spirits remain under the earth; if they come up
onto the surface of the earth, tell it to Mai-Terè.
Mai-Terè is strong, he will conquer them. Pondo-
Sünkü shall make fast the sun and the moon, Mandi-
Shirè shall keep watch upon earth and heaven. Mai-
Terè will hold the evil far away from the good. Mandi-
Shirè, do thou battle; when strength comes to thee,
then call upon me; do not cast one away (merely) because thou holdest him to be evil. Among those who
survive the dead let everything be equal. If thou
holdest a prince to be evil, do not therefore reject
his subjects as being evil. If thou holdest a prince to
to be good, do not therefore take to thyself all his

subjects as being good; instruct mankind in all that is good. Teach him to angle for fish, teach him to catch fish in nets, teach him to shoot squirrels, teach him to pasture cattle, lead him into all that is good, as though it were I myself."

Thereupon God withdrew.

Mandi-Shirè remained behind, made a fishing-rod, and angled; he spun hemp, he made nets, he made boats and fished with the net; he made a gun, he made powder and shot squirrels. Thus he went before them in all that was good, according to the word of God; he instructed them in all things. One day Mandi-Shirè spoke: "Today the wind will carry me away." There arose a whirlwind and carried Mandi-Shirè away.

Yapkara spoke: "Mandi-Shirè has God himself taken away; do not seek for him, you will not find him. I am God's messenger and I will also return; I will go to the land where God (now) lets me dwell. Do not let up in that which you have learned; this is strength given by God."

Saying this, he went away.

The names of two other of these saints, beside Mandi-Shirè, are nothing more than names of Buddhist teachers; while Shal-Jimè is obviously Yima-Kshasta, Jemshid in the sacred Iranian traditions.

The Turkic and Mongolian variants of this story, which is interesting in many respects, are indicated and in part are translated in extenso in the works of Veselovskij (Razyskanija XI: 23ff and XX: 107ff). We have no reason to linger over them, and shall confine ourselves to but a few episodes from them. Thus for instance in the stories of the Altaian Tatars and Mongols, collected by Potanin, we encounter an interesting detail; namely, that the initiative in extracting the earth from the bottom of the water and the animating of man's body belongs to Erlik, not to God. Another variant of the same tale contains a detail which we have met in the Ukrainian legend, namely, when the two demi-urges fell asleep on the newly-constituted land, Shulmus (a doublet of the devil) thought of throwing them into the water; but, in measure as he carried them, so did the land grow. From the details of the Volga Finno-Turkic tales it will suffice to note the episode where the devil-demiurge was formed from the spittle which God spat into the primeval sea (Veselovskij, Razy-skanija XI: 8). This detail recalls a similar trait in the

Bulgarian tale (of Drinov) and in a Grusian variant (as we shall see below).

Setting forth the Turko-Altaian and Mongolian variants of the legends that concern us, Veselovskij offers the following: "The (Russian) Raskolnik colonization may have brought (this narrative) to the frontiers of Russian soil, where it could be taken over and appropriated by the natives; but another assumption is also possible, as we have already surmised: for instance, in their development the Cheremiss, Mordvian, etc. and southern Slavic legends may have belonged at first to one and the same region and to one and the same religious world-view. The Bogomils may possibly have inserted into the cycle of their dualistic traditions some non-Slavic traditions which fitted their aims, and the Cheremiss and Altaians may have received back their ancient cosmogonic myth, heightened by Christian heresy and the apocryphas." (Razyskanija XI: 32).

Of the unsustainable character of the Finno-Turkic hypothesis for the origin of the tales that concern us — which hypothesis Veselovskij himself actually repudiates — we have already spoken.

There remains to say a few words about the proposition that the Altaian Turks and their neighbors, the Mongolians, may have appropriated the dualistic tales from the Russian Raskolniks, who in turn had gotten them from the Bogomils. It seems to us that Veselovskij errs when he arranges in one series the tales of the Volga and Ural Finns and Turks with the tales of the Siberian Turks and Mongols and their Chinese neighbors. The first are often so like the Russian tales that they truly may be acknowledged as taken from the Russian, even though it is possible to assume the opposite borrowing. This closeness is quite natural, if we keep in mind the ancient borrowing activity between the Russians and the natives in the Volga-Ural region; while it is otherwise in the Upper Yenisei and Mongolia. Here the Russian colonization has penetrated but very slightly into the country of their non-relatives, while in Chinese Mongolia there is no colonization at all. Here too the dualistic tales are not as similar to the Russian as for instance the Cheremiss or Mordvian are.[3] The tales have rather a Buddhist-Lamaistic coloring than a Christian.[4] The name of the supreme god in the Altaian-Turkic tales obviously is Iranian. The episode of how people came into being recalls the same episode in the

Bundahish. Although some details in this tale recall the story
of Adam, as told in the Bible, there still is no necessity for
assuming that it was taken from Russian Christian sources, since
these details could have penetrated Central Asia by a more direct
route. Above all, the Hebraic traditions basically approach the
Chaldean and even the Iranian, which must have spread eastward
as well as westward; next, we must not lose sight of the fact
that Biblical stories, even in their latest Christian-Gnostic
construction, could have penetrated Central and Northern Asia
much earlier than the Russian influence; namely, by way of the
Manicheans and the Syrian Nestorians; the latter of whom have
left us some inscriptions in the Syro-Yeniseian region, and who
laid the foundations of the Uigur-Turkic and Mongolian alphabet.

Particularly the tale of how the snake tempted people to
eat the fruit of the well-known sacred tree must have existed
among the Chaldeans, as can be seen from a figure atop a
Babylonian cylinder which is now in the British Museum: under
a fruit-tree there stand a man and a woman, and behind the
woman a snake.[5] If we take into consideration the close connection of their cultures and the historical conditions for instance,
the great height of the Babylonian culture as compared with
the Hebrew — we must assume that the Chaldeans did not
obtain these tales from the Hebrews; consequently their basis
could have spread eastward from Chaldea too, and quite independently of Biblical influence.

Moreover, the whole story in the Sibero-Turkic tale of the
forbidden fruit is told in a different spirit and with different
details, and not as in the Bible. Thus, for instance, in the
Turkic tale the prohibition to eat certain fruits is motivated
with concepts that completely agree with dualistic ideas: the
people are allowed to eat from the fruits on the eastern branches
(those of Ormuzd), but are forbidden to taste of those on the
west (Ahriman's).

Finally, according to the Bible, God (Yahweh, Elohim),
after the Fall from Grace, does not want people to be like him;
while in the Turkic tales, on the contrary, Ormuzd says that,
had the people continued to submit to him, they would have become like him.

These, and other details like them, give us a basis for
considering the above-cited Altaian tales to be completely independent of the Biblico-Christian sources, and to see in them

remnants of the ancient Irano-Chaldean sources which have
penetrated into the Altaian region long before the Russian colonization; in all probability, along with Manicheanism.

In the Assyro-Chaldean region itself, the traditions like
those above must have sustained a strong pressure from the
side of the Christian and Moslem conceptions, which were
supported by a literate clergy; and so they could not be preserved as intact as might be. Their elements none the less are
discovered in the oral literature of the representatives of the
various sects in Mesopotamia and in the regions neighboring
them on the north, and in part even in their books, which however are still but slightly explored.

In the region of the same ancient Chaldea there is a sect,
that of the Mandeans, which call themselves Sabaeans, the
Christians of John the Baptist, etc. Their sacred book is the
so-called Liber Adami or Codex Nazaraeus. It is known in
Europe, among other things, in a Latin translation by Norberg
(1815 et seq.). A goodly number of their oral tales are recorded
by the French vice-consul in Mosul, N. Siouffi, and published
in his book, Etudes sur la religion des Soubbas ou Sabéens,
leur dogme, leurs moeurs (1880). Furthermore, they are the
subject of an investigation: Les Mandaïtes, leur histoire et
leurs doctrines religieuses, by Babelon, in Annales de philoso-
phie chrétienne (October, November 1881). Most recently there
has appeared a German attempt to investigate the religion of
the Mandeans, by W. Brandt: Die Mandäische Religion, ihre
Entwicklung und geschichtliche Bedeutung (Leipzig 1889). It
is useful also to remember the article of Kessler: Mandäer,
in vol. IX of Herzog's Real-Encyclopaedie der protestantischen
Theologie.

The religious conceptions of the Mandeans are very confused,
for they are a mixture of polytheistic, dualistic, and monotheistic ideas, which took shape under influences both old and new,
beginning with the Chaldean and down to the Moslem. But their
conceptions of the creation of the world are distinctive, with
their obviously dualistic character; and they contain the very
elements of that mixture of Chaldean and Iranian ideas and
imagery about which we have spoken above, and especially all
of the essential elements which enter into the composition of
the Slavic and Turkic dualistic tales, although in other combin-
ations.

According to the cosmographies of the Mandeans, the earth lies upon the water; and according to their cosmogonies, the light god charges the creation of the world upon another, whose condition is ambivalent, but who emerges from the region of darkness and resembles Ahriman more than he does Ormuzd. (He bears various names and now is sometimes identified with the Archangel Gabriel.) According to some tales, the creation of the world begins with the light spirits being doused in the water, or one of them in the dark, damp abyss (Babelon, October, p. 88).

According to various Mandean tales, the creation of the world begins thus: The creator condenses a part of the turbid water and throws this beginning of dry land into the ocean (Brandt, pp. 35, 53); or else he dries up the damp abyss and obtains a dust, which forms the germ of the earth (Babelon, ibid.)

Man is created, according to the teachings of the Mandeans, with the participation of the dark powers: the (female) representative of the darkness, Rukho (something similar to the Chaldean Tiamat) along with her seven progeny, proposes to God that they create man; and they actually create his body (Brandt, p. 36); or else the creator himself proposes to the seven planets (which in the Chaldeo-Iranian system are counted among the evil powers, in contraposition to the stationary stars) that they create man (Babelon pp. 93-94). Only, these creators are not capable of giving a spirit to the human body they have made.

The spirit is inserted by the pure representative of the light beginning, just as in the teachings of the Gnostics and the Manicheans (Brandt 72, Babelon 94, Matter II: 143-444). [6] After this the seven demonic beings create the false religions and the harmful animals (Brandt 38).

The Yezids, who are called by the Christians and the Moslems "Devil-worshippers," belong in nationality to the Kurds — an Iranian tribe — and live in Upper Mesopotamia and in Turkish and Russian Armenia.

They are described by various European writers, e.g. Layard (in his book, Nineveh and its Remains, 270-309); by Siouffi (Notice sur la secte des Yézides, in N. Journal Asiatique August, September 1882); by the Russo-Armenian scholar Eliazarov, whose essays, unfortunately, are not to hand; by Eliseev (Sredi poklonnikov diavola, in Severnyj Věstnik, January, February 1888); by Ed. Kovalevsky: Les Kurdes et les Jésides, following his own observations and those of Messrs. Eliazarov, Eliseev, in Bulletin de la Société royale belge de géographie, 1890, #2.)

We also find small notes about the Yezids in N. Journal Asiatique II (1873): 393-395: Notes sur les sectes dans le Kurdistan, by Gilbert; and ibid., I (1880): 78-83: Une courte conversation avec le chef de la secte des Yézides, ou les adorateurs du diable.

At all events we must remember that the beliefs of the Yezids are still not sufficiently known: their books still have been read by no scholar; in their conversations they do not like to talk about their religion, and in the presence of strangers they are not communicative.

The Yezids are called devil-worshippers because they worship not only God but another person also: Maluk Taus, who recalls somewhat the Hebrew Satan, as he was formed after the Babylonian exile under Iranian influence, and the Satan of the Christian and Moslem beliefs.[7]

The Yezids say that their Satan really sinned before God, by revolting against him; but he has expiated this sin with his long wandering over the world, and has received back his former place near God (Gilbert, 394). Others say that Maluk Taus still is unforgiven, but he will be forgiven (as some Persian books also teach); but for the present we must bow to him, just as for instance we are obliged to honor some royal favorite who for the moment has fallen out with the king.[8] (Ed. Kovalevsky 179-180).

This sort of Yezid belief is probably derived from the Zervanitic tales, which do honor to Ahriman and ascribe to him a significant place in the creation of the world. In harmony with the present Asiatic, much more unitarian conceptions of the creation, the beginnings of which conceptions we still find among the Zervanites, the Yezids affirm that God first created everything beautiful and light; he peopled the world with houris and sinless angels; and had decided to take a rest, when Maluk Taus appeared before him and said to him: Thy creations are not complete, for everything in them is of one shape; but there can be no balance in the world without darkness, likewise day cannot exist without night or fragrance without stench, angels without demons and their houris. Good and beauty can be born only of contrast.[9]

God replied: Go and create!

Maluk Taus hurled himself from heaven; with the shadow of his wings he covered the earth and the universe, and with his icy breath he created evil in contrast to good, cold to heat, storm to fair weather. Poisonous growths covered the earth, beasts of prey took their abode in the forests, monsters appeared among people, and sin developed very quickly. Then there appeared also the evil spirits and the tempting demons.

When God saw that he had ruined his world, he was angry, and cursed Maluk Taus. The latter fled to the earth and began to wander from one region to another. Every one who recognized him scolded him, drove him away and would have nothing to do with him. Only the Yezid people have taken him in, and therefore in their time they will be rewarded.

In these legends, obviously Iranian themes are developed. But among the Yezids there are other legends, in which it is clear that they are mixed with Chaldean ascetic conceptions.

Such legends we encounter in the collection of Siouffi.

In one of them there is told that "In the beginning the world was an ocean, in the midst of which was a tree created by divine power.

God lived on this tree in the form of a bird, for an unknown number of centuries. In a different region, far from the other, was a rose bush covered with flowers. On one of these flowers was Sheik Sinn or Sheik Hassan el Baseri, whom the Lord had caused to emanate from himself.

After that, the Lord created from his own reflection the Archangel Gabriel, also in the form of a bird, and placed him beside himself on the tree. After a little he asked him, "Who are you and who am I?" Gabriel answered, "You are you, and I am I." With this proud answer the archangel wished to give God to understand that each of them had a special importance and that he, Gabriel, could consider himself the peer of his creator. When the Lord heard Gabriel's answer, he became angry, he pecked the archangel and drove him from the tree. Gabriel flew off and began to cut the air with his wings.

He wandered into every part of the world. He flew for several whole centuries, but finally he tired and returned to alight again on the tree. God again asked him, "Who are you and who am I?" The exile again answered the same as before, and again the Lord pecked him and drove him from the tree. Again he wandered over the desolate expanse, without a chance

to rest. Once, when quite exhausted, he flew without realizing
it, close to the rose bush of Sheik Sinn; the latter exclaimed,
when he saw the archangel, "Where are you going and why are
you whirling about so?" The bird answered, "Far from here
there is a tree, and on the tree a bird; and whenever I try to
perch on that tree, the bird drives me off." "What has it said
to you," asked Sheik Sinn, "and what have you answered, that
it behaves thus towards you?" Gabriel then told him his conversation with God. So Sheik Sinn taught him how to behave if
he wished to get over his trouble. "Go back to the tree," he said
to him, "and when God again asks you the question, you answer,
"You are the creator, and I am your creature. You are the
guardian by your preëminence, while I am your protégé." Then
he will let you sit on the tree with him."

The archangel returned to God, who propounded the former
question. The answer conformed to the counsel of Sheik Sinn,
and then God asked Gabriel who had taught him to say that.
Gabriel said, "A person whom I found on a rose bush in the
midst of the ocean." "Aha," said God, when he knew who it was,
"that is our Lord Al-Uarkani."[10] (Siouffi explains that this name
is composed of an Arabian noun meaning leaf, and signifies one
who lives in the foliage of the rose.) Gabriel then remained
with God.

In this tale the ancient cosmogonic notions have been subjected to strong influence from the side of Moslem monotheistic
ideas; in spite of this, they are very clearly visible. The inde-
pendence of Sheik Sinn's condition and the respect with which
God speaks of him, when he calls him "Our Lord," show that
Sheik Sinn must at first have been some deity, something like
Zervan, while God and the archangel Gabriel must have considered themselves his progeny, like Ormuzd and Ahriman.
The conversation of these two deities in the form of birds reminds us of the antagonism of the Iranian gods and especially
the conversations between God and Satan in some of the Slavic
and Turkic tales.[11]

From the explanations of Siouffi it is seen that the archangel Gabriel in this story replaces Maluk Taus, Satan or
the shaitan, as the Christians and the Turks call the devil when
they speak about the beliefs of the Yezids.

Farther on Siouffi reports to us, as a continuation of the
foregoing, a story which probably was independent, for it does

not agree fully with that given above: God created other persons
and a large number of angels, called to himself Sheik Sinn and
made a boat. Three more persons had been created at that time:
one carried the boat on his head, another steered it, and the
third pushed it. Six people sat in the boat and went over the sea
many centuries. During the time of that long sailing these six
persons began to wrangle because each claimed that he was
God Almighty. This anarchy would have shortly become the
occasion for resentment. Then the six took counsel and saw
that not all six could be of equal worth and power. They finally
decided to acknowledge as almighty whoever had power to con-
dense the water until it became firm and whoever should be able
to raise the heavenly dome. After this resolution each began
to try to make the water firm. For this purpose they began to
swim one after the other, but all their efforts proved vain. The
turn came to God: he spat upon the world and the water immediately turned into dry land. At this time, when the change was
taking place, the ocean was strongly stirred. A vast quantity
of thick vapor emerged from its depth and covered the whole
region so that everything was plunged in darkness.

Then God, to save the world from this evil, created the
two great lights, and also the stars, and the world became
light. After that the Lord created the heaven and generated
paradise and hades.

This story too has some traits in common with the Slavic
and Turkic dualistic tales (the gods floating on the ocean,
swimming in the water), even though we do not meet in it one
essential detail: the diving into the water.[12] The dualistic
character of this tale has been worn down, and perhaps only
latterly has it been restored; which is likely, if we give attention to the note of Siouffi, namely, that on the place where God's
spittle is supposed to have fallen the Yezids to this day gather
the sacred dust from the ground; which dust they call the "dust
of Sheik-Aadi." Sheik-Aadi, even if now he is a Moslem saint
(the Yezids often go to his grave and keep by it the image of
Maluk Taus in the shape of a bird), is none other than the
personification of Maluk Taus.

According to the beliefs of the Yezids, when Sheik Saadi
appeared in the guise of a Moslem saint, he said, "I existed
also in times past, and now I am coming among you." (N. Journ.
Asiatique II (1880): 81). In this way the world-creation appears

in the tale above as the work of Maluk Taus, the Yezid devil.

In the following Yezid tale, recorded by Siouffi, this is said about the creation of man: God said later to his companions, "Behold, now we have made heaven, earth, paradise and hell.[13] Now we need subjects. I propose that we create Adam; but for this purpose one of you must agree to be incarnated in him. Who of you will decide to do this?" But no one consented.

Then God said to Sheik Sinn: "You shall be incarnated in Adam." The Sheik demurred again, and begged God to spare him from this affair, saying that he did not want to live in a kind of being which with all its progeny would be subject to all kinds of sins and should commit all sorts of errors. "Thus it must be!" insisted the Lord. "If this is after all inescapable," replied Sinn, "I shall yield, but under one condition only: that you yourself shall accompany me to the body that you are going to create and shall put me into it; and also that you shall create a paradise for a habitation of the first man in whom I am to live." These conditions were accepted. God then mixed a paste out of the four elements, fire, water, air, earth. Out of this paste he made a statue in the form of a man and placed Sheik Sinn in it. At that moment Adam began to live and entered into paradise. After that, from the remains of the paste God created Eve, whom Adam embraced as soon as he saw her. Something like this tale of the creation of man we see in the beliefs of the Mandeans. Farther on we shall encounter the same episode in the Bulgarian Bogomil Gospel of John.

If we place this tale beside the teachings of the Gnostics and the Manicheans, we can conclude that in the original source of the Yezid tale the creator of man must have been the devil. The soul of man is part of the basic deity, or that first Adam who proceeded from the deity and fell into the primeval matter.

And so, in the Yezid tales we find material from the Iranian and the Chaldean cosmogonies, and likewise Gnostic and Manichean beliefs which have also entered into the constitution of the Slavic and Turkic dualistic tales. Of course, the Yezids have altered these materials markedly and have put them together in a different way, under the pressure of monotheistic ideas, especially Moslem.[14]

This pressure, obviously, must have been weaker in the more northern regions, in Trans-Caucasia; we find therefore

among the Grusians and their kin the Suanitians some tales
which occupy an intermediate position between the Yezid and
the Slavic.

Since in many respects the Grusian-Suanitian legends
resemble strikingly the Bulgarian, we shall present their con-
tents as fully as possible.

In one Grusian tale the following is told: At first the universe was covered with water. God, creator of the world, was
in the Samkarian rock. Once he came out of it and threw himself into the water. The water was cold for him: he gasped and
two tears fell from his eyes. These tears turned into the archangels Gabriel and Michael, of whom the former always stands
on God's right hand and the second on his left.

God sank farther and farther into the water. Then the
archangels Michael and Gabriel seized hold of him and drew
him out. The three of them had somehow or other to annihilate
the water and uncover the dry land. With this object they
began to blow on the water and so they reached the bottom of the
sea and stood upon the sand.[15] Here they saw tracks of some
unknown being. God said, "Come, let us follow these tracks;
whose are they and where will they lead us?"

The archangels agreed, they started on the spoor, and so
they came to a large blue stone. When they had lifted the stone,
Samoel[16] jumped out and seized God by the throat and almost
choked him to death. God was distressed and asked aid of the
archangels; but not even they were able to free God. There
was nothing else to do, so the Lord began to beg Samoel thus:
"Ask what you will, only let me go!" Samoel answered, "I
want nothing but to become your brother." God consented. So
Samoel let him go and went his way. God and the two angels
were left. They began to part the water from the land, but
they could accomplish nothing. They raised a wall between
the water and the dry land, but the pressure of the water always
caused the wall to collapse and the water again united with the
dry land. The three were distressed: they saw that their
efforts were in vain, and they did not know what to do. The
archangel Michael said to God, "Go to your brother Samoel;
maybe he can tell you what we should do." God consented.
The angel went to Samoel and told him the object of his mission;
and indeed Samoel gave him advice on what to do. "Tell my
brother God," said Samoel to the archangel, "that you must

make stones as many as possible and build the wall all three of
you, and again tear it down. Carry on this building-up and
tearing-down until you are sick of it. Then prepare two trum-
pets, put them side by side, and you two angels blow into them
with all your strength; blow a loud blast and the dry land will
become free of water; the former will remain, and the latter
will go to one side." The angel Michael thanked Samoel for
his counsel, returned to God, and told him all. God and the
archangels carried out Samoel's counsel; the water withdrew,
and the dry land showed. When the water had parted from the
earth, God in seven days created all the animals and man.

The first people were Adam and Eve. God took dirt, breathe
a soul into it, and Adam and Eve appeared, but they were both
blind. The archangel Michael showed them where to live, told
them not to listen to any one until he came back; and he went
away. Adam and Eve were left alone. At this time Samoel
came to them in the form of a billy-goat and said to them, "Why
do you stay here? Here by you is an apple tree, climb into it
and eat its fruit and you will be able to see.[17] Eve harkened,
climbed into the tree, picked an apple, took a bite, and passed
the apple to Adam. So both received sight and were ashamed
of their nakedness. After a while Michael came, called Adam
and Eve, but they did not disclose themselves because they
were naked. The angel understood the situation, and told them
that it would have been better if they had waited; and he went
away. After this the progeny of Adam and Eve multiplied in
the way we now see.[18]

When this all had happened, Samoel again went to God, and
begged him as a brother to divide to him what was his due. God
was not willing. "Well then, why did you become my brother?"
Samoel asked God. "If you won't give me anything else, at
least give me some sapitseri." (The translator of this myth
explains that sapitseri was the sort of thing which caused whatever a man sacrificed to God or gave as a memorial to the
dead to belong instead to whoever possessed it.)

God gave Samoel the "sapitseri." Samoel swallowed it and
went back to Hades. A long time passed, and Christ was born.
He took with him all that was alive in the world, from man to
reptiles, and went to Hades. When Christ saw Samoel, he
seized him by the throat, squeezed him and made him render
the sapitseri.

Later there follows a rather original trait: how Samoel tried to hold Christ in hell, yet Christ managed to escape. However, we omit this detail because it is not relevant to our topic.

Another variant relates somewhat concisely, yet with some interesting details, the first part of the legend, and correspondingly the story of the appearance of Christ is told more fully:

Michael and Gabriel were going about the world. The earth's crust at that time was so soft that they sank into it to their knees, even though they had on their feet a kind of skis. Before them a round stone kept rolling on the ground. God said, "This stone irks me; I am going to break it!" The angels opposed him: "Don't — we'll regret it afterwards!" they said. God would not heed them; he kicked the stone and broke it. Out of the stone sprang Samoel; he seized God by the throat and started to choke him. God was in distress and said, "Just let me go and I'll give you anything you want." Samoel said to him: "Give me either the visible world, or the invisible, eternal one." God yielded him the eternal world. Samoel left God on earth and went away. The angels said to God: "We have done ill. From now on the soul of every man will be in the hands of Samoel; the memorials made to the dead will be his; and when the people know this, will they do you honor? Come on," said the angels, "let us hunt out Samoel and tell him, when God has a son to relinquish to him the eternal world."

"Hm, if it suits God to have a son, let the eternal world be his," answered Samoel.[19]

The angels returned to God, and they all went on with their business. On the way they came upon a stream, in which Mary was washing something. The archangel said to God: Breathe your spirit into my palm, and I will go and put it into Mary's mouth." God agreed. The angel took God's spirit in the hollow of his hand, carried it to Mary, and put it into her mouth. Instantly she felt herself pregnant. When she went home, she told her mother everything. The latter questioned her about everything, and when she learned what it was all about, she told her to be careful.

Mary became pregnant, and she bore Christ. After his crucifixion and death, Christ descended into hell to Samoel and brought out the souls of all the people, except the soul of Meka (?).[20]

In both variants of the Grusian legend, especially in the second, the agreement with the devil is presented just as in the Bulgarian folktale, i.e., the agreement is reached between God and Satan, not between Adam and the devil, as in the written Slavic apocryphas (Tixonravov: Pamjatniki otrečennoj russkij literatury I: 16-17; Pypin: Ložnyja i otrečennyja skazanija o vetxozavĕtnyx licax i sobytijax po rukopisjam soloveckoj biblioteki 93, 211-212. Russkij Filologičeskij Vĕstnik IV (1887): 174; Cf. Joannis Apocryphus Liber I, in Codex Apocryphus Novi Testmenti I: 888).

This peculiarity of the Bulgarian and Grusian tales and the Slavic and Finno-Turkic ones similar to them, justifies our considering them to be older than the written Slavic apocryphas and closer to the Iranian tales about the agreement between Ormuzd and Ahriman (Bundahish ch. 1, Minokhired, in Spiegel: Die traditionelle Litteratur der Persen, 95-98, 143), than they are to these written apocryphas. Only in the third Grusian tale[21] known to us does the agreement become one between Adam and Samoel.

The Suanitian tale[22] has preserved some further traits even older than the details in the Grusian legends. Thus, e.g., it says in them directly that God and Satanail were co-eternal.

There was a time, says the Suanitian legend, when there was neither heaven, nor earth, nor what now is to be found in them. And everything was covered with water, with a sea. In the midst of this sea rose a high rock and in this rock was the Lord. It irked God to sit alone on the rock, therefore he opened it up to 12 versts of spread and jumped out. Then he dried up the water and mixed the water and the earth that were around the rock; after that he divided them in two: from the one part the Lord made the heaven, from the other he created the world for the people and animals. But as yet there were no living creatures; then God began to cry of vexation, and one tear dropped from his right eye and from it came the archangel Michael, then a tear fell from his left eye and became the archangel Gabriel. Much time went by. At God's command many people were created. God and his angels walked together over the creation. For a long time they rode over the world on their handsome horses, everywhere they dried up the water for the people, and at last they saw a huge boulder white as snow, and they started in its direction; but the [three] travelers did not take God to that rock, but led him by a different route.

They came back again, but again the angels did not guide him
to that rock. Then the Lord said to his angels, "This looks
like your cunning, that we have not been able to go to the rock,
else we should have found it." The angels said, "Very well,
let us lead you to the white rock; but we think that this will
bring us only evil and woe, if we see the white rock." They
came to the rock. God struck the rock with his whip, the rock
shattered and from it there jumped out the devil and immediately
grabbed the Lord's horse. God called the angels to help. Then
they surrounded Satan and began to ask him who he was, or
whose master he was. The devil said to God, "You and I —
both of us were in the rock; you and I — both of us are of one
breed [family, descent-Guarish] I am the heart of the rock,
like yourself, therefore divide to me part of the creation. God
proposed that the angels adjudge the request of the devil. They
divided everything into three parts: on one side they separated
all living people, on another the souls of the dead, on the third
all beasts and birds.

God chose for himself the people and the animals, while
the Devil took the soul of man. But the angels added one condition; they said to the devil, "Satan, don't be too joyful. Know
that the soul of man shall be in your hands only until God has
a son, who shall save all the souls of the dead from your kingdom." The devil answered that until God should have a son,
much, much time would pass, so it would yet be enough for him
to deceive many human souls.

The devil made hell and surrounded it with a wall. Only at
one place was a hole left, through which there entered the souls
of the people. In hell there were many devils who in the presence of the oldest devil tortured the souls in every way. Much
time went by, and the soul of man was ever tormented in this
way; but the time came for the son of God to be born. God
took pity on the souls of the people, and God wished to fulfill
the condition which had been agreed upon between himself and
the Devil when they divided the world between them. God and
his angels gathered for council; all expressed their opinions;
one angel said that he knew a righteous married couple who
had a daughter named Mary. Then God took an apple, breathed
into it his spirit and gave it to the angels. They took the apple
and went to Mary's house. Mary was a pure virgin; at that
time and in that place there was none other who in all respects

was as good a girl as Mary. The angels went to Mary's home, but she was not there: she had gone with the laundry to a spring. So the angels went there. The archangel Gabriel, without showing himself, threw the apple that God had given him. Mary took the apple and bit into it three times; yet there remained no signs of the bite on the apple. Finally Mary put the apple into her bosom. At that the archangel Gabriel appeared to Mary and said to her: "Rejoice, Mary, because when you bit the apple the Holy Spirit entered into you. You shall conceive and shall bear a son; he shall be Christ; therefore be sanctified and keep yourself from everything that God does not like." Mary wondered at these words of the angel, but afterwards she praised God greatly.

And indeed, as the angel had said to Mary so it happened. When her time came, Mary bore a son in Bethlehem city. Christ grew very rapidly; he was so intelligent that all wondered at him. One day Christ was baptized and began to teach the people, and he always taught good things. He clearly expounded to the people who is the true God and what are his laws (his will). Twice in his preaching Christ said to the people, "I shall undergo much pain until I shall have transferred the sand." But the people did not understand these words. Then a youth said, "Teacher, we have not understood what your words mean, therefore tell us clearly and we shall complete your work." Then Christ said, "All of you follow me." The people started after him. Christ led them all to hell, tore it down, brought forth from thence the dead, and led them into paradise; God had prepared paradise previously. In this way Christ defeated the Devil and destroyed his kingdom of hell. O most glorious Christ, what marvelous works thou hast wrought!"

If we examine the Grusian tales adduced farther back (which are not hard to restore completely by comparing their various details) and if we compare them with the Bulgarian and the Altaian, we can reach the following conclusion:

The Grusian-Suanitian tales are straight popular reflections of the written dualistic tales: of the Chaldeo-Arabian teachings, and those which have grown from their beginnings — the Gnostic, Marcionite, Manichean, etc. We see in the detail of God's weakness the same that we encounter also in the yielding quality of Ormuzd before Ahriman, or that of the First Eon (the First Adam) before Satan. These vestiges show that a distinction has been made between the supreme God and the creator of the visible world (the Old Testament God of the Gnostics, etc.); they indicate also the existence of the conception that the world had been given over to the power of the Devil until the appearance of the supreme God or of the First Eon in the person of Christ, etc. Only that the imagery answering to these doctrines has been messed up in the folk tales; so that, for instance, the role of the supreme God turns out to be divided here between God and Samoel.

At all events, the very existence of such tales in Trans-Caucasia where it has not been possible for either Slavic or Turko-Altaic influence to penetrate, speaks clearly in favor of the fact that these tales cannot be of northern provenience — whether Slavic, Finnic, or Turkic — but must on the contrary be referred back to more southern sources that are at the same time older than the Slavic apocryphas; above all, to Irano-Chaldean sources.

And since the Trans-Caucasian tales are in many respects like the Slavic, even to the point of identity, especially with the Bulgarian and the Turkic, we have still another basis for considering these latter also as being derived out of Irano-Chaldean sources.

However, we must observe that in the Trans-Caucasian tales there is lacking even the faintest trace of the episode of the diving by the creator-Devil into the sea for the purpose of obtaining the basis of dry land from there; an episode which is met in the Mandean tales. The separating of water from dry land on the advice of Samoel reminds us only distantly of the episodes in the Slavic and the Turkic tales about the participation of the Devil in the creation of the world. We think that this difference between the Trans-Caucasian tales and the Slavic and the Turkic has come about as the result of atrophy in the corresponding episodes of the Trans-Caucasian legends, under the influence of the mountainous and continental condition in the life of the Grusians and the Suanitians.

This atrophy we observe also in the second Bulgarian tale (of Drinov) even though its kinship with the first (from Obsht Trud) is subject to no doubt whatever.

Since it is the second Bulgarian tale which includes in its ending details extremely similar to the details of the first and also with the details of the Trans-Caucasian tales, and at the same time its beginning is close to the Trans-Caucasian legends, we are even more justified in assuming that in their original form the Bulgarian and the Trans-Caucasian tales were almost identical, and therefore they must have come from a common source.

Farther along we shall attempt to trace the provenience of the Slavic tales and especially the Bulgarian under the influence of the Trans-Caucasian; but for the present we shall say only a few words about the analogies which the Yezid and Trans-Caucasian tales have with some Slavic conceptions, and especially with the Galician Christmas carol about the creator-doves.

We cannot but recognize that there is similarity between these doves and the creator birds in the Yezid tale; and furthermore we cannot let go unnoticed the coincidence of the rock out of which (according to the Galician Christmas carol) there were created the heaven and the heavenly lights, with the rock in which (according to the Grusian-Suanitian tales) there dwelt originally God and Satan (the blue stone in the Galician kolyada; lapis lazuli, which was thus valued in Chaldea). The refrain in the Galician song, "Breathe, O Lord, with Thy spirit upon the earth," corresponds to the breathing of God and the angels in the beginning of the first Grusian variant, and to Christ's breathing upon the sea in the Syrian tale in Socin's collection.

Finally, we must also set the Yezid episode of Sheik-Sinn's residing (we have already spoken of his supremacy as deity) in the calyx of a rose, beside the Ukrainian tales which tell that first the Lord created a woman for Adam out of a rose; and when Adam would not agree to have such a wife, the Lord said to him: "I shall give her to be the mother of my son." (Čubinskij, Trudy Ekspedicija, etc. I: 145, 146). Sheik-Sinn also recalls the king of the two-headed giants, to whom the Lord turns for counsel as to how to conquer the giants. The king advises him to destroy them with a flood (Rulikovskij, Mythes et croyances paiennes de l'Ukraïne, in Revue internationale, Juin 1888.)

These are all trivia, but they show that the Mesopotamian and Trans-Caucasian conceptions have exercised some influence upon the Ukrainian, even if in the case given it is hard to determine the route of that influence. As regards the tree on which the creator-doves sit in the Galician Christmas carol, many surmises have been expressed up to now; among others, by Veselovskij in his works on the luminous tree.

We shall remark that comparisons of the different conceptions of the luminous tree for the purpose of ascertaining their genetic connections, must give precedence to the Chaldean and Iranian images, for they are the oldest and are attested documentarily.[23]

From the Magyar gypsies there is recorded a tale of the world-creation which offers some traits which are similar to the Yezid and Grusian tales, and also with the Altaian. It contains, however, some details which are still more ancient and in all probability Iranian:

When there was nothing on earth anywhere, except a vast quantity of water, God decided to make the world, only he did not know how to begin the job. As he was disgusted because he could not find a way and still more because he did not have a brother to consult with, he threw into the water the stick on which he leant when he walked on the clouds. As soon as the stick struck the water there grew up immediately in that spot a gigantic tree, the roots of which reached down to the depths of the sea. On one of the branches of the tree sat the devil, who at that time was white, like the man God later created.

"Dear God, dear brother," cried the devil, and smiled, "I am really sorry for you. You have no brother nor companion. All right, I will be your brother and companion."

"Oh, that cannot be," answered God, "you cannot be my brother; no one can be my brother. Be my companion."

Nine days after this conversation, when the Lord still had not created the world, because he did not know how to go about it, he remarked, as he was once walking with the devil, that the latter was not very well disposed towards him. The devil, who was not stupid, remarked that the Lord did not trust him and so he said, "Dear brother, don't you think we are not quite compatible? Command and create one more, to make three of us."

"That is easily said," God replied, much injured, "Make another? — Make him yourself, if you are so clever."

"Yes, but I am not capable of such work," said the devil, "else I long ago would have created the beautiful broad world. What is the use in my desiring, when I do not know, dear brother, how to undertake the matter?"

"All right," said the God, as he pondered and scratched the back of his neck as though he had remembered something. "I will create the world, but you must help me. Come, let's get busy and not lose time: do you plunge into the water and bring me a handful of sand, that we may make the earth from it."

"Is that so?" said the devil, pretending to be a nit-wit. "But how will you make it? I don't understand."

"I will pronounce my name and the sand will itself round up into a ball," answered God, "but hurry up and get the sand."

The devil dived into the water and said to himself, "Oh, I am not so stupid as to let some one else create the world. I will create it myself by pronouncing my own name."

When the devil had reached the bottom of the water, he grabbed some sand in both hands, but as he pronounced his name he had to let go the sand, as it burned his hands. When the devil returned, he told God that he could not find any sand.

"Go and search, but bring what I commanded you."

For nine days he kept saying that he could not find any sand. He lied, for he always sought to create a world himself from the sand in the water, so he pronounced his name; but each time he burned himself. The sand became hotter and hotter and began to burn him so that he at last became black, like coal.

When the Lord saw the devil, he said to him, "I see you have turned black. You have been a bad companion. Hurry and bring me sand from the water, but do not pronounce your own name, else the sand will burn you completely."

The devil dived into the water and did as he had been told.

God took the sand, pronounced his name, the world was created, and the devil was very pleased.

"Here," said he, as he sat down under a shady tree, "under this tree I am going to remain; and you, dear brother, go and find yourself a home elsewhere."

This impudence so enraged God that he said, "Ah you vagabond, wait, I'll teach you sense; get out of here!"

At that a huge bull jumped out of the bushes, picked up the devil on his horns and ran off and away with him.

The devil from fear and pain began to yell, so that slivers splintered from the tree and turned into people.

Thus the Lord created the world and people in it, with the help of the devil.[24]

In spite of the fact that the Magyar and Transylvanian gypsies live as neighbors of the Slavs, and are even surrounded by the latter, still the assumption must be excluded that the Gypsies may have borrowed from the Slavs the tale just given, in view of the great differences of this tale from the Slavic.

At the same time, traits in the Gypsy legend such as the Devil emerging from the abyss (cf. the Grusian tales), his wrangling with God on the tree, the fire in the depth of the water (cf. the Yezid traditions), bring this legend into propinquity with the Mesopotamian and the Trans-Caucasian; also the provenience of the people from the tree, and the bull that routs the Devil (this bull resembles the wondrous animals, among their number also the bulls which defeat the creatures of Ahriman in the Bundahish ch. XIX), tell clearly of the Iranian influence in the Gypsy tale.[25]

It is obvious that the Magyar and Transylvanian Gypsies have brought the base of the above-given tale from their sojourn in Irano-Mesopotamian regions.

The beginning of the Gypsy tale (with the luminous tree that grows out of the water, and the Devil on the branch) evokes the impression of something more intact and older than does the corresponding Yezid tale. It reminds us of the lotus in the midst of the ocean, and the gods sitting on it, in the Indian traditions;[26] so that the Gypsy tale can show us how the base of the tales that concern us penetrated from India into the Irano-Chaldean region.

At all events, these data, which occur in the tales set forth from the Altaians, the Mandeans, the Yezids, the Trans-Caucasians, and the Gypsies, it seems to us, are enough to convince us that the base of the dualistic tales that concern us took shape definitively precisely in the Irano-Chaldean portion of Hither Asia.

Notes

1. At this place, Dragomanov (pp. 290-293) partly abbreviates the story. I have substituted from Radloff's original a complete translation; the tale is too remarkable for any lesser

treatment in the present circumstances. It contains at once an apparently primitive fundament; plus detritus from Manicheism, Christianity (presumptively, Nestorian), Buddhism (Lamaist); possibly Zervanism and/or Mazdaism. EWC

2.   In the Bundahish the fruits of the tree of Paradise represent ten human races.

3.   The latter are set forth in full in the essay of Veselovskij, and this leaves nothing to be desired. Since it is impossible for us to enter into details with regard to this material, we direct the inquiring reader to the work itself by the illustrious Russian academician.

4.   We must remark that Mani in fact was acquainted with Buddhism; the Babylonian-Iranian theosophist even borrowed some features from it. — Kessler, in _Realencyclopädie d. prot. Theologie_ IX: 231.

5.   This sketch is reproduced in the atlas accompanying the mémoire by Lajard "On the Cult of Mithra" (Pl. XVI, #4) and in many other essays; among others, Lenormant: _Histoire ancienne des peuples de l'Orient_, ix éd., t. I.

6.   The author of the "Philosophoumena" says: "The Chaldeans call Adam the man whom the snake produced. He lay without movement, without life, and without breath, like to the heavenly Adam, until the latter bestowed a spirit upon him." Lenormant: _Les origines de l'histoire_ etc. I: 41.

7.   The Yezids avoid mentioning this god by name. Maluk Taus properly is the name of a figure that they carry at the time of their religious processions.

8.   These Yezid conceptions of Satan remind us of the conceptions of some Zervanites, who say that Ahriman at first was good and served Ormuzd. Spiegel: _Alterthumskunde_, II: 178.

9.   Eg. Kovalevsky, 174-175.

10.   See N. Siouffi: _Notice sur la secte des Yézides_. _Journal Asiatique_, 7ᵉ sér., t. XX (1882): 252-268. On p. 253, loc. cit., Siouffi says in a footnote: "Sheikh Sinn is also a deity to the Yezids, since he derives his existence from the divine nature itself. For this reason he is superior to the other heavenly beings of which we shall speak later (i.e., to the 'other three beings' later created by God: EWC). His real name is Sheikh Sinn; but when they speak of him to people of alien beliefs, the

Yezids call him Sheikh Hassan el-Bassri, a Moslem person who died in sanctity in the second century of the Hegira . . ." — EWC

11. In a Great-Russian tale the Evil One says to the Lord: "Hah, let us become born-brothers; you be the younger and I the older." The Lord smiled. "Let us be, then, Lord, equal brothers." The Lord again smiled. "Very well, Lord, you be the older while I be the younger." "Take me," said the Lord, "by the arm above the elbow; now squeeze my arm with all your strength." The Evil One seized the Lord by the arm above the elbow, he squeezed with all his strength but he only tired himself out. But the Lord simply stood and smiled. Then the Lord seized the devil by his arm — and the devil doubled up. The Lord signed the devil with the cross and the devil fled to hell. (Buslaev'': Očerki etc. I: 457. Cf. Afanazjev'': Nar. russkija legendy #14; cf. farther on, the Gypsy tale.

12. We must notice, however, that according to the Slavic and Finno-Turkic tales, the floating in the water does not produce the creation of the world, but the creation of Satanail. Thus for instance in a Mordvin tale (Veselovskij, Razyskanija XI: 12) and in an Ukrainian, instead of floating the Lord breathes on the foam (ibid., 59). According to the Grusian legends, of which more anon, the angels proceed not from God's spittle but from his tears. In the Bulgarian tale of Drinov, the devil proceeds from God's shadow.

13. This phrase gives us grounds to assume that the companions of God had taken part in the creation of the world just as in the Zend Avesta the angels of above, the alshostands (sic; saoshyants? EWC) help Ormuzd to create it. We must remember that in the Biblical tale not only the name of God (Elohim) stands in the plural number but in some places even the corresponding verbs and pronouns for this name are put in the plural.

14. As we leave here the Mesopotamian region, let us note a fragment of the Chaldean oceanic cosmogony encountered in the oral traditions of the Syrian Arabs. In the publication of Prim and Socin, Der neuaramäische Dialect des Tür Abdin (II Th. Uebersetzung 219) we read: "The whole world was a large sea and Christ floated on the water in the form of a bird. At last he breathed on the sea and because of this the heaven raised up from the sea, and even a multitude of fishes rose with it. Christ changed these fish into stars."

15. Such are the representations reached by a constant anthropomorphizing of the old cosmogonic idea of the significance of the wind in the creation of the world.

16. Samoel, the angel of death in the Old Testament Hebrew apocrypha, identified with Satan.

17. We have seen in the Bulgarian tale that the billy-goat was a creature of the devil; Satan straddles him when he travels to God. In the traditions of many other peoples also the billy-goat is considered to be a creature of the devil (see the Ukrainian tradition in Čubinskij: Trud" Ekspedicii I: 79; the Great-Russian in Sadovnikov": Nar. skazki Samarskago kraja, 251; the German in Brothers Grimm: Haus- und Kindermärchen #148 et al.). In the Moslem traditions, the angel of death appears to Adam in the guise of a billy-goat (Weil: Biblische Legenden der Muselmänner, 42). These conceptions may have something in common with the Chaldean conceptions of the goat, who was considered an enemy of the vine and the palm. The two together were identified with the tree of life by the Assyro-Babylonians. (Cf. Lenormant: Les origines de l'histoire etc. I: 75-83; — V. Lajard: Recherches sur le culte etc. de Venus, atlas, Pl. II contains an interesting figure copied from a Babylonian cylinder which shows a goat attacking the tree of life; also a dog that, it seems to us, has been set to defend the tree. Cf. also Pl. IV #12.

18. This tale of the sin-and-fall departs strongly from the biblical; its character approaches rather the tale in the Bundahish and the Turko-Altaian.

19. Sic; the abruptness of the phrasing suggests that the printer may have omitted a passage from Dragomanov's manuscript. EWC

20. Who this Meka was, the transmitter of this legend does not say.

21. All these Grusian tales are taken from the Sbornik materialov dlja spisanija městnostej i plemen Kavkaza X: lxxv-lxxx.

22. Sbornik materialov etc. X: II: 245-251.

23. Cf. the Assyro-Babylonian figures farther along in the appendix; also in the Bundahish, beside the passage adduced above, Ch. XXVII, which has the tree in the midst of the sea of Vurukasha and containing the seeds of all plants and of the primeval sea (sic; possibly an error of print. EWC). The ancient Chaldean conceptions of the luminous tree were preserved among the Mandeans, whose sacred book promises to the righteous that they shall see the tree Setarvan (the "shady") in the region of the higher life. . , . "Et qui abhis vindicaverit, ascendet

Vitam Summam in suo habitaculo visurus, vitem puram <u>sam</u> et <u>starvan</u> arborem, unde extitit, visurus, vitem Schor visurus, et in hujus cacumine, tractu et celsitudinae habitaturus" (Norberg, Codex Nasaraeus III: 68-69). The translator of the Mandean sacred book defines Setarvan as "arbor umbrifera in sede Vitae Summae vigens" and the name of the vine <u>Sam Gufno</u> as "vitis fragrans, in sede vitae summae vigens" (op.cit., onomasticon 117, 111). The vine that corresponds to the plant <u>haoma</u> (Asclepia acida) of Aryan tradition is the tree of religious ecstasy and corresponds to the tree of the knowledge of good and evil. In this way the Mandean tradition has preserved clearly the difference between the trees, which in the Hebrew traditions are somewhat confused with each other (cf. Genesis 2: 9-17, 3: 3-20).

24. Journal of the Gypsylore Society II: 2, April 1890: <u>Gypsy Anecdotes from Hungary</u>, by Władg. Kornel; p. 67-68. One variant of this tale is inserted into the collection of H. v. Wlisłocky: <u>Märchen und Sagen der transilvanischen Zigeuner</u>, Berlin 1886: "#1: Die Erschaffung der Welt." This variant is shorter. We cannot resist the opportunity to express the wish that it might occur to some one to occupy himself particularly with collecting songs and tales among the <u>Bulgarian</u> gypsies.

25. This influence can surprise no one after the many facts which have been collected, e.g., by Kunavin while investigating the Gypsies in Europe, Asia, and Africa (cf. Kounavine: <u>Materials for the Study of the Gypsies</u>, by Dr. A. Elysseeff, in <u>Journal of the Gypsylore Society</u>, 1890: 2-4; out of the <u>Izvestija Imp. Russko Geogr. Obšč</u>. 1882). In the Gypsy stories, even the name of Ahriman is encountered: Anromori (Angromainyus). Clear traces of the Iranian legend of Vara (paradise) and Jemshid and the Irano-Chaldean conceptions of the luminous tree are seen in the tale of the Transylvanian Gypsies: Wisłocky op.cit. #7: <u>Der Baum, den allerlei Jammer traf</u>.

26. Compare also the tale of the deluge in Wisłocky, op.cit. #3: <u>Die Sündflut</u>; which is an obvious reflection of the Indian variant of the Chaldean tale.

4 The dualistic legends of the world-creation may have entered Bulgaria from Hither Asia via an Armenian-Paulician medium. — The position of the Bulgarian dualistic tales with respect to the Bogomil cosmogonic conceptions; the Bogomil cosmogonies according to Zigabenos and the "Liber S. Ioannis." — The tale of the diver-Satanail in the Great-Russian apocryphas "About the Tiberian Sea" and the "Bundle of Divine Books". — The problem of the relation of these apocryphas to the ancient Bulgarian apocryphas. — No Serbian tale is known of a Satanail who extracts lumps of dirt for God to create dry land. — The peculiarity of the Serbian tales about the devil-Duklyan diving into the sea. — The Bulgarian and the Ukrainian variants of these tales. — The Iranian tales about the diving of Afraziab. — The shattered Slovene tale of the creation of dry land out of a grain of sand extracted from the sea-depths.

As we now start to review the distribution of the dualistic tales of the world-creation in Europe, we must first of all dwell on the Bulgarian tales. It is readily noticeable that all their component elements are found in those Asiatic tales which we examined above, especially the Mesopotamian and the Trans-Caucasian. To be sure, the oceanic motifs (in the latter) have by today become attenuated, as compared with the Bulgarian legend in "Obšt Trud"; but it is important that the antagonism between God and Satanail and the birth of God's son who is to recover for God's side the upper hand, in the Trans-Caucasian legends, is told so similarly to the Bulgarian that inevitably it raises the question of borrowing. This question must be answered in favor of the assumption that the legends have passed from the Trans-Caucasians to the Bulgarians; for it is known documentarily that not only the teachings of the dualistic Armeno-Paulician sect passed into Bulgaria, but that these Armeno-Paulicians themselves were more than once transplanted by the Byzantine emperors to Bulgaria, where they preserved until recently even the name of Paulicians; even though now they are Bulgarians in language, and since the XVII century Catholics by faith.[1]

However, it is necessary to determine exactly to what degree the above-given Bulgarian legends resemble the teachings
of the Paulicians and the Bogomils who were connected with
them. As far as these teachings are known to us from the
Mediaeval monuments, especially from those with a condemna-
tory character, and also from the apocryphas constituted under
the influence of those teachings, we must admit that the Bulgarian oral dualistic legends coincide with these teachings only in
the general situation and not in details. The general situation
is this: a belief in the dualism of creation, in which the creation
of the visible world is ascribed to Satanail.[2] From there on,
the particular concepts of the world-creation are quite unlike in
the oral Bulgarian legends and the Paulician-Bogomil variants
respectively.

In the Bulgarian oral tales, we may say, the dualism has
weakened even more than among the moderate Bogomils, who
recognized the Devil as not being co-eternal with God but as a
later creation of his who had revolted against him. Thus, in
the second Bulgarian tale (Periodičesko Spisanie VIII (1884):
124-126), in the beginning God is alone, and later the Devil
takes shape from his shadow. In the first tale (Obšta Trudə),
which is fuller, there is to be sure no word as to the creation
of the Devil by God; yet instead the initiative for creating the
world belongs to God, while in this the Devil plays a servant's
and even a lowly role. But in the development of both tales we
are struck squarely by the fact that God is weaker than the Devil,
who is defeated only by God's son in the first tale, and by the
angel in the second.[3] It is obvious that the base of the oral Bulgarian variants has developed rather parallel with the teaching
of the Bogomil bookmen, under the influence of the oral imports
of the Hither-Asiatic cosmogonic legends into Bulgaria, than
directly out of the beginning of the teachings of these bookmen;
even though at last one may entertain alteration of these teachings
in the popular medium, especially after the time when the organ-
ized Bogomil religious communities were stamped down. Were
not the similarity of the Bulgarian oral tales with the Hither-
Asiatic so extensive, we would have ascribed to the latter circumstance a greater significance than to the former; but because
of that very resemblance we ascribe the greater significance
to the former.

In any case it is very curious that the literary sources from which we can obtain a conception of the Paulicians, the Bogomils furnish us nothing like the tale of the creation of dry land out of lumps of soil which the Devil brings to God from out of the sea. Of these sources, the condemnations by the Byzantine theologian Evtimeus Zigabenus, and the apocryphal Revelation of John the Theologian, which was popular among the Bogomils and their western brethren, possess an especially legendary element.

Zigabenus wrote a special treatise "Against the Bogomils,"[4] where he set forth their teachings in considerable fullness; chiefly about a moderately dualistic agreement according to which Satan was the son of God, just as was the Word-Christ, and also the older; but he rebelled against his Father, while the Word-Christ remained faithful. Because of his rebellion Satan was expelled down out of the upper world which God had created. According to Zigabenus, the Bogomils say: "From the time that he was thrown down out of the upper world, Satan was unable to sit upon the waters, because the earth had not been built and was not to be seen. But since he had divine form and creative capability, Satan called the angels who had fallen along with him, instilled them with boldness and said to them: 'God has created heaven and earth; come, let me also make, as another God, another heaven and everything else along the same line.' And he said: 'Let there be solid ground,' etc. Later, when he had made Adam out of earth mixed with water, he stood him on his feet; his moisture gathered in his right foot and ran out onto the ground through his sole and instantly took the form of a snake. Satan took his spirit ($\pi\nu\epsilon\hat{\upsilon}\mu\alpha$) and breathed life into the body (of Adam); but the spirit passed through empty space in the right foot (of Adam's body) and the sole and entered the exuded moisture; which then, as soon as it had obtained life, became a snake and began to slither like a snake. . . Then Satan sent messengers to the good Father and begged him to send out his spirit ($\pi\nu\omicron\acute{\eta}\nu$); promising him that, if the man should receive life, he would be the common property of both of them, and that his progeny should fill the places from which the (rebel) angels had been expelled. . . Then Satan created Eve, united with her and begot Cain, while later from Adam there was begotten Abel."

Here is memorialized that in the very beginning, before Satan, there had been the water, and this suggests to us to some

extent the first Bulgarian tale. But subsequently, between the
Bogomil tale of Zigabenus and the Bulgarian there is nothing in
common; even though on the other hand the Bogomil story of the
creation of man resembles the above-cited Mesopotamian. As
among many other peoples, among the Bulgarians there is a
story of how Satan vainly struggles to create man; a tale at long
last inspired by the same conceptions as the Bogomil, but with
a different plot: the Devil, wishing to create man in the likeness
of the creations of God, spun out the wolf, but even that he could
not animate. God advised him to exclaim, "Arise, eat me!"
The wolf came to life and bit the Devil's foot.[5]

The narrative also in the Bogomil Revelation of John bears
the same kind of relationship to the Mesopotamian and Bulgarian
tales.

This curious apocrypha was found in Latin translation among
the Provençal exponents of Bogomilism: among the Cathari in
Carcassonne; it had been brought over from Bulgaria in the XIII
century; so testifies a contemporary heretical bishop. This
apocrypha was first printed in the treatise of Benoit: Histoire
des Albigeois et des Vaudois en Berbets (Paris, 1691. I: 285-
296; later it was reprinted in Thilo: Codex apocryphicus Novi
Testamenti (1832. I: 884ff). Not long ago Döllinger presented
a different although very similar version from a Vienna manuscript, with variants from still another (Döllinger: Beiträge
zur Sectengeschichte des Mittelalters. Dokumente vornehmlich
zur Geschichte der Valdesier und Katharer; 85-98). Thilo already expresses the assumption that the Greek transcript (perhaps the original) of this apocrypha is presented from the manuscript Προσελθὼν ὁ ἅγιος Ἰωάννης τῷ κυρίῳ εἴπων, which according to one catalogue (J. Aloys. Mingerelli, Catalogum Bononiae
a. 1784 editum, p. 289) at the end of the XVIII century was to be
found in the Venetian library of St. Mark. But for a wonder, no
one has tried up to now to locate and edit this register; so it
is not known but that by now it has faded out.[6]

This apocrypha, called by Thilo Liber S. Ioannis apocryphus,
and in the Vienna transcript The Questions of John (Ioannis et
Apostoli et Evangelistae Interrogatio in coena sancta regni
coelorum de ordinatione mundi et de Principe et de Adam), sets
forth in the form of answers by Christ to John's questions at
the Last Supper, the history of the creation of the world, Christ's
incarnation, and the coming Last Judgment. In its general

framework, the Bulgarian oral tale in "Obšt Trud" can be likened to this apocrypha as being its oral parallel. Yet in the matter of details, there is a great difference between these two tales.

In the Book of John, the Beloved Disciple first asks his teacher who will betray him. The answer includes the remark that Satan will enter into the betrayer. Farther on the disciple asks, "Before he fell, was Satan in glory by thy Father?" Christ answers, that Satan had administered heaven while he, Christ, sat by his Father; that Satan had thrown himself from heaven into the nether regions (de coelo in infinimum), and from there he had raised himself to the throne of the invisible Father; that he had finally thought to place his throne above the clouds and to become equal with the Most High (similis Altissimo). "When Satan hurled himself into the air (in aerem), he said to the angel of the air, 'Open me the gates of the air,' and the angel opened to him the gates of the air. When Satan had hurled himself lower, he found the angel who rules over the waters (tenebat aquas) and said to him, 'Open me the gates of the waters.' And when he had hurled himself farther, he found the earth covered with the waters. As he wandered about, he found two fishes lying on the waters; and the fishes were tethered like oxen before the plow, and they supported the earth at the command of the Invisible Father. When Satan had plunged farther, he saw hanging clouds which supported the sea (pelagum maris), and, plunging farther, he found his hell (suum ossop, in Thilo; suum infernum, in Döllinger); i.e., the fiery Gehenna; and he could go no farther because of the raging fire.[7] The Satan returned, with rancor in his heart, and raised himself to the angel that was above the air, and to the one that was above the waters, and said to them: 'All this is mine; and if you will serve me, I will place my throne above the clouds and will become equal with the Most High, and I will take the waters from this solid (earth) (substraham aquas supra firmamentum istum), and will gather the sea into other places, and after that there will be no water over all the surface of the earth, and I will reign with you forevermore.'"

Farther on it tells how Satan seduced the angels of various heavens to his side, by reducing in their bills the tribute which they had to pay to God in the form of grain and olives; then, how God punished the seduced angels. Farther on, John puts a new question to Christ: Where did Satan find himself after his fall? Christ tells how the light of his glory was taken from Satan's face, and that his face became like tempered iron,[8] and his shape became like that of a man; how he threw himself down to the firmament, carrying on his seven tails a third of the angels; but he did not find the earth here, and cried out to God, "I have sinned!" etc. God took pity on Satan and gave him the world for seven days. During that time Satan created the visible world after the words of God the Invisible Father (per praeceptum Patris invisibilis). Two parts of the water rose into the air, and from the last third Satan along with the angels of the air and the water made the sea.[9] Commanding the angel of the waters to step upon the fishes, Satan raised up the land and then created out of the crown of the angel the moon and the sun; out of the stones, fire; out of the fire, the stars; then, angel-spirits, thunder, rain, hail, snow; and placed angels over all this. Then he commanded the earth to bring forth all kinds of living things, trees, grass; and the sea to bring forth fishes and birds. Then Satan thought of making man, to serve him. He made him of slime, after his image, and commanded the angel of the second heaven to enter the body of the man. He made another body with the form of a woman and commanded the angel of the first heaven to enter it. The angels wept a great deal, and Satan commanded them to have carnal union (carnalia opera facere); but they did not know how to commit this sin. So the originator of sin built a paradise, sent the people there and commanded them not to eat anything in it. Then he entered alone and planted rushes (arundineum), and from his spittle he made a snake and commanded it to lurk in the rush. Then Satan (who in this tale of paradise is now called Diabolus) commanded the people: "Eat all kinds of fruit in paradise, but do not taste of the fruit of iniquity" (de fructu iniquitatis ne comedatis). Then the malicious Devil entered the snake and seduced the angel that was in the body of the woman by putting into the woman's head sinful desire and inflaming her passion. The Devil came out of the rush and coupled with Eve by means of the snake's tail. Therefore his descendants are called not sons of God but sons of the Devil and of the snake, who accomplish the will of the Devil to the end of time. Then the Devil put desire into the head of the angel who had become Adam, and the two of them (Adam and Eve) being of one desire, began to produce sons of the Devil and the snake to the end of time.

Answering to the further questions of John, Christ explains that the kingdom of Satan shall last seven days, that is seven centuries, and that at last, in order that the malice of the Devil shall be convicted before the people, God sends him (Christ) here. Satan, knowing this ahead of time, furnishes the staff of Moses that had been saved up to this time, that Christ may be crucified. Before Christ's appearance in the world, God sent his angel to Mary, to receive him into herself. Farther on, Christ says that he entered Mary through her ear and came out of her the same way. And Satan sent his angel, the prophet Elias, who began to baptize the people with water and called himself John the Baptist. Christ explains to his disciple the difference between the baptism of Satan with water and his own — a spiritual baptism; between the matrimonial life of the disciples of John the Baptist and the non-matrimonial life of the truly-blessed, and replies at considerable length to the question of the end of the world and the Day of Wrath; which moreover he depicts in agreement with the canonical gospels.

The tales of the Book of John are obviously constituted in the same spirit as the tales of the Bundahish and the Manichean books, with which they have some details in common (the entering of Satan into heaven, the truce with God, the creation of the world). But of course the Book of John has its differences, which are Judeo-Christian and heretical in particular. With the Bulgarian oral tale in "Obšt Trud" the Book of John agrees in the details of Satan's diving, in the extraction of the earth (but it is the whole earth, as in the Indian cosmogonies), in acknowledging the time until Christ's resurrection as that of the kingdom of Satan, in indicating antagonism between Mary and Christ on the one hand and John the Baptist on the other. But first it can be said about these details only that they have been selected in one and the same fashion; second, that here the analogy between the two tales, the apocryphal and the oral, ends It is clear that the oral tale has not proceeded straight from the written apocrypha, but only out of a medium subjected to the same influences as in the case of the apocrypha. If the Bulgarian oral tale came to Bulgaria out of the Asiatic homeland of the Paulicians, it has traveled somehow from mouth to mouth, independently of the written apocryphas like the Book of John.

In the same way there must have penetrated into the Bulgarian tale other details also, which we find in the various European and eastern apocryphas.[10]

We consider it especially important that in the Johannine book there is nothing like the characteristic plot which we find at the beginning of the Bulgarian tale, and which is so developed in the dualistic tales of the world-creation among the Russian Slavs, and also among the Turkic peoples of Asia; as we have shown above. There are no traces of this plot in the other Slavic apocryphas too, which can be derived out of Bulgaria with certainty. Only in one apocryphal monument, considerably wide-spread in northern and eastern Russia, is there found a likeness to this plot. We refer to the monument known under various names: "About the Tiberian Sea," "About the genesis of the heaven and the earth," "The story of the creation of the world," "The Bundle of Divine Books," etc. The fuller transcripts of this interesting monument are printed by E. Barsov'' ("About the Tiberian Lake") in "Čtenija v Imper. Mosk. Obšč. Ist. i Drev. Rossijskix'' II (1886), and by Močul'skij in Russk. Fil. Věstn. 1887 #4 (Istoriko-literaturnij analiz'' stixa o Golubinoj knigě; there is also a separatum), from a manuscript by V. Grigorovič'' in the XVIII century. Beside this, a variant of Barsov's tale, from a fragment of the manuscript Povest'stgo. Andrěę so Epifaniemu o voprosěxǝ i otvětexǝ from the XVII century has been edited by Porfirjev'' in Apokrifičeskija skazanija (Vetxago Zavěta) po rukopisjam'' Solovetskoj Biblioteki (87-89); and Pypin has presented in Istorija slav. literatur'' I: 379-81 rather large extracts from the manuscript Svitok'' božestvennyx'' knig'' (Bundle of Divine Books) which gives us a variant of the Grigorovič'' manuscript. The fullest consideration of this monument has been given by Mochul'skij (op.cit.) and by Veselovskij (in his researches, already alluded to, into the present stories); the latter has had a new variant communicated to him by Porfirjev'', and he adduces a full bibliography on the subject.

Above all, we shall concur with the regret expressed by Veselovskij that this interesting monument still has not been edited and analyzed critically. Hence even its provenience is still uncertain. Veselovskij divided the various known transcriptions of this monument into two categories: in the one the tale begins immediately by telling how God appears on the Tiberian sea (which has the role of a cosmic sea), and there meets the

Devil (in Barsov", Porfirjev"); in the other division (in
Grigorovič"-Močul'skij, Pypin) this encounter is placed as an
episode in the tale of the creation, and that after the tale about
the separation of the Son of God and of the Holy Spirit from the
Lord Savaoth, and about the creation of the world by Jesus
Christ at the command of the Father (a heaven on iron pillars,
lakes, clouds, light, wind, paradise, etc.).

This particular episode of the encounter of the Lord with
Satan is especially interesting to us because of its likeness to
the oral narratives we have been examining; we submit it here
under title "About the Tiberian Sea."

When there was no heaven, nor earth, then there was one
Tiberian sea, and shores to it there were none; and the Lord
descended in the air over the Tiberian sea and the Lord saw
on the sea a goldeneye (clangula) swimming, and this goldeneye,
Satanail, was born of the froth of the sea. And the Lord said
to Satanail, as though he had not seen him: "Who art thou?"
And Satanail said, "I am God."[11] "And how dost thou denomin-
ate me?" And Satanail answered, "But thou art God of God(s),
and Lord of Lord(s)." Had not Satanail said these words to the
Lord, then the Lord had thereupon rooted him out from the
Tiberian sea. And the Lord said, "Satanail! Dive into the sea
and bring me up earth and flint." Satanail obeyed the Lord and
dived into the sea and brought up earth and flint. And the Lord
took the flint from Satanail and broke it up on the ground, and
in his right hand did the Lord keep some for himself, while that
in his left did the Lord bestow upon Satanail. Farther on comes
the provenience of God's angels out of blows rained with a cudgel
upon God's rock, and the Devil's angels out of the piece of flint
given him. We shall have more to say about this tale later.

In Porfirjev's transcript, the conversation of God with the
diving-bird (the golden-eye) and the creation of earth are given
thus:

. . . "And God said, 'Who are you?' The bird answered,
'I am God.' 'And who am I?' The bird answered, 'Thou art
God of God(s).' God said again, 'Whence art thou?' The bird
answered, 'Ego ex infimis.' And the Lord said, 'And whence
am I?' The bird answered, 'De superis.' And the Lord said,
'Da mihi ex infimis.'[12] And the bird dived into the sea and
brought up froth like slime and brought it to God. And God took
the slime in his palm and strewed it hither and yon and it became

earth. And God commanded that it dry up to rivers and springs; (thus has a continental people distorted the conception of a drying-up of the earth out of a primordial ocean!). And God took the bird and called its name Satanail, and be thou the chief of my heavenly forces, above all elders. And after that God created the heavenly powers. . . ."

In the "Bundle of Divine Books" edited by Pypin, Satanail extracted sand and flint from the sea and "cast it abroad upon the Tiberian Sea, saying: Let there be earth both thick and wide."

There follow upon these tales, in the several transcripts of this document, various episodes more or less common to the Judeo-Christian cosmogonies, especially to the apocryphas: establishment of the earth upon whales, creation of Adam from various pieces, rebellion of Satan against God, sin-and-fall of Adam and Eve, Adam's bill (his note) delivered over to Satan granting dominion over the earth, etc.

In assessing the present situation of the question of this monument, we may say that the tale which begins with the meeting of God with the diver-Satan on the Tiberian sea formerly constituted a separate narrative. It has subsequently been placed in the tale which began with the lineage of the Divine Trinity. However, we shall not insist too strongly upon this point; nor do we undertake to ascertain at what time or in what place the tales of the Tiberian sea and the Bundle of Divine Books were constructed.

Pypin places the Bundle with the episode of the Tiberian Lake squarely in the history of Bulgarian literature, along with the Bogomil apocryphas. The other investigators are close to this opinion.[13] Were this to be correct, we should have to admit that the Slavic oral tales of the diving of Satan into the sea for the purpose of extracting lumps of dirt, have proceeded straight from out of the Bogomil stories. But the question of the provenience of the narrative about the Tiberian sea and of the Bundle does not seem to us as clear as that — it seems to us that the relations which various scholars have indicated between these narratives and unquestionably ancient apocryphas, such as the Besĕda trexə svjatitelej (Discourse of the Three Prelates), which is known also in a Bulgarian edition (printed by Novakovič in Starine, v. VI), are too thoroughgoing.

Of course, this Besĕda (Discourse), as well as the monuments analogous to it, such as the Church-Slavic Kniga bytie

nebesi i zemli (edited by A. Popov in Čtenia v Mosk. Obšč.
Ist. i Drevn. R., I (1881)), the Serbian Slovo za neboto i zemjata
(fragments in Jagić, in Archiv. f. sl. Phil., I: 95), or the
Bulgarian Slovo, "Skazaniye o Bytie" (in the manuscript of
Novakovič it stands before the Discourse, and occurs, according
to the indication of Močul'skij, also in the manuscript of Drinov;
see R. F. V. 1887 #1, 123, p. 155) to some extent treat of the
same eschatological questions as do the story of the Tiberian
sea and the Bundle: of the world-creation, the greatness and
fall of Satanail, of the whales upon which the earth rests, etc.
The ancient monuments mentioned contain also some cosmogonic
notions, which are constituted in the same way as the stories of
the Tiberian sea and the Bundle, or else actually inserted into the
Bundle. The following places are of this sort: (1) in the Serbian
Slovo of the Heaven and the earth: "Out of what was the earth?
Out of the slime of the water." (2) in the Bulgarian Discourse:
"Learned question: Out of what did the Lord create heaven and
earth? Answer. From the watery scum and curd were heaven
and earth created." (3) in the Russian transcripts of this same
Discourse: The Lord did command to gather slime of the sea
and create the earth. (Porfirjev", Apocrif. skaz. o novozav.
litsax" i sobytiax" po rukopisjam" Solov. bibl. 385); which place
may also be interpreted as meaning that God commanded some
one else, e.g., Satanail. But these details are far from the
circumstantial and vivid tale in which God meets the diver-
Satanail and gets him to obtain the beginning of the earth out of
the water. It still does not follow from these similarities, even
though they are the basis of the story which we encountered in
the narrative of the Tiberian Lake and in the Bundle, that it
occurred inevitably in the ancient Bulgarian apocryphas. The
narrative of the Tiberian sea and the Bundle of Divine Books
have up to the present been found only in (northern) Russia
and in late transcriptions (XVII-XVIII centuries); so that it is
very possible that these narratives were first written down in
Great-Russia, and in late times at that, e.g., no earlier than
the XVI century, out of materials both written, e.g., Paleae and
the Besěda trexə sviatitelej, as well as oral. The latter could
have been supplied particularly by the tale of the Bird-Satanail,
which probably had been diffused among the Russian Slavs long
before. And this tale could easily have reached the Russians
either from the south, from the Bulgarians, or directly from

Asia Minor via the Black Sea; or else via the Caucasians, or
again from the east, from the Turanian peoples.

In order to resolve these questions and to eliminate the
doubts which are raised by the narrative About the Tiberian
Sea and the Bundle, it is necessary to investigate minutely all
variants of these stories, both paleographically and linguisti-
cally. Thus it would be determined when they were constituted
and how they are related to the Balkan Slavic apocryphal writings.
Of course such labors can be undertaken by the scholars who
live in Russia.

In investigating the question how the tale of Satanail's diving
into the sea to obtain particles of earth is related to the written
Bogomil apocryphas, the following must not be forgotten: While
this tale is so widespread among the Russian Slavs that it is
told with all these details, in Bulgaria it constitutes but an
episode; and a brief episode at that, in one story, and it has
been written down in but one variant. This is characteristic.
We must remember that the motifs of the apocryphal writings
are in Bulgaria very usual, and are well known: a shining example of this is furnished us by the story of the Holy Cross and
Lot. . . . Next, it strikes us squarely that among the Serbs a
tale on the theme of Satanail's extracting dirt from the sea with
God's help is not to be found; in spite of the fact that in this
region Bogomilism was considerably widespread and has left
observable traces in the ancient writings and the oral literature.

Usually Afanasiev, Veselovskij et al. juxtapose to the Bulgarian episode of Satanail's extracting the earth in the "Obšt
Trud" tale and the Russian tales like it, the Serbian stories that
resemble the episode in the Bulgarian story in Periodičesko
Spisanie (vid. supra); i.e., the legend of the struggle between
the archangel and the Devil for possession of the sun, printed
by Karadžić, Srpske narodne pripovijetke, 2nd ed., 91-2, and
the Montenegrin song of the struggle of King Duklyan (Diocletian)
with John the Baptist for the crown, printed by Karadžić, Srpske
narodnie pjesme II: 81-4 (reprinted in Bezsonov: Kaliki perexožie
I: 601-5). We shall permit ourselves the judgment that this
juxtaposition has been made without sufficient basis: it has been
done solely on the basis that here too there is a diving into the water
as in the dualistic tales of the world-creation that have been
reviewed, and also that here too there is presented a struggle
between divine and demonic beings.

But where do not such struggles occur? And as for the diving, it is not merely a matter of this alone, but of its motives, and of the plot in which we find it. Between the motives for the diving in the Serbian stories and in the episode in the tale of "Obšt Trud," and also between the plots of these two narratives, there is nothing in common. In the Serbian story, the devils, when they left God, grabbed the sun, which the king of the devils bore stuck on the end of his spear. The earth began to pray to God that it was being scorched by the sun, and God sent the archangel to take the sun from the king of the devils. The archangel began to go over the earth with Satan. Once they came to the sea and started to bathe. The king of the devils stuck his spear with the sun into the ground. The archangel proposed to Satan that they dive, to see who could dive deepest. The archangel dived and brought up sand in his teeth. When it came the devil's turn, he created a crow out of his spittle and placed it to watch the sun while he threw himself into the sea. But when Satan had dived in, the archangel made the sign of the cross over the sea, so that the sea iced over; he seized the sun and flew godward. The crow began to caw, the devil heard it, but he could not break through the ice; he dived back down into the depth, took a stone, and with it he broke the ice and took after the archangel. But the latter already had one foot in heaven, so that the devil succeeded only in biting a piece of flesh out of the other sole. To comfort the archangel, God promised that all people should have hollowed soles.

We find the same plot at the base of the Montenegrin song; except that here the place of Satan is taken by King Duklyan, and the place of the sun by his crown. Duklyan drinks water on the sea, along with his brother-bondsman John the Baptist. John proposes to Duklyan that he play with his crown, while he (John) play with an apple. John threw his apple, and it fell into the depth of the sea. John began to cry, but the king said, "Don't cry, dear bond-brother; I will find your apple; but don't you take my crown." John swore by God that he would not take the crown. So the king plunged into the sea, and John flew up to God in heaven and asked, "Eternal God, and most holy Father, is it all right for me to swear falsely and make away with the king's crown?" The Lord answered him, "O John, my faithful servant! Three times you may swear falsely before me, only do not swear with the use of my name." When the king brought

the apple, John again threw it into the sea, and three times he
swore before God that he would not steal the king's crown. The
king again plunged into the sea, having left on the shore a "bird
with an evil voice." John covered the sea with twelve sheets of
ice. Beyond that, the tale runs as in the narrative. The song
approaches the latter also in the feature that John brings to
heaven the bright sun, which, obviously, king Duklyan's crown
had become.

It is clear that these Serbian stories have the same basis as
the episode of the angel's taking from the Devil the latter's receipt for the earth (for Adam's inscription given to the Devil,
see Tixonravov'': Pamjatniki otrečennoj literatury I: 16-17;
Pypin: Ložnyja i otrečennyja knigi russkoj stariny, in Pamjatniki
starinnoj russkoj literatury, edited by Gr. Kušlev'': Bezborodko
III: 2, 5; Porfirjev'': Apokrifičeskija skazanija o vetxozavětnyx''
litsax'' etc. 93, 211-212; Močul'skij, in Russk. Fil. Vestn. IV
(1887): 174; the Bulgarian tale cited above from Period. Spis.
VIII (1884)). But these stories, except for the diving, have nothing in common with the tales of Satan's extracting earth for
constituting the dry land. And the one feature of diving is not
enough for us to identify the two legends.

For comparison with the southern-Slavic stories of how the
angel seized a precious object from the Devil when the latter had
dived into the sea, there are three variants written down from
Russian Ukraine. One of these is recorded in Novgorod, Northern
uyezd, in the government of Chernigov, and is reprinted from
the Černigovskija Gubernskija Věbomosti (Feb. 13, 1892) in the
Etnografičeskoe Obozrenie, #'s 2-3 (1892) (books XIII-XIV),
sec. I, p. 253:

Once the devil stole somehow from the Lord his heavenly
power. (What this "heavenly power" was, the woman who nar-
rated the tale could not explain). . . . And the devil made himself a crystal heaven[14] (the heavenly power helped him to do
this), and he lived in the heaven. And Lord God says to the
archangel Michael, "How shall we get the heavenly power away
from the unclean spirit?" And Michael answers him, "Suppose
I go and maybe I can steal it from him." God gave him permission, and he went. He comes to the devil, and says, "Do you
know the breadth of the world and the depth of the sea?" The
breadth of the world the devil knew, and also its height, but he
had forgotten the depth of the sea. The Lord God had made him

(forget it) at that time. So the devil dives to measure the depth.
And Michael grabbed the heavenly power and took a breath to
flee. The devil measures (the depth of) the sea, but does not
realize that the Lord God has covered the sea with ice. The
devil wanted to come out — he looks: the ice won't let him.
For a long time he suffered until he had broken through the ice;
he came out of the sea, but Michael was already high up, he
could hardly be seen. Then the Lord God said to Michael,
"Strike him with the heavenly power!" Michael struck him, and
the devil was shattered into small drops, so for forty days it
rained."

The other variant was recorded in Kiev from the account of
a peasant who had wandered much in the southern Ukrainian
districts (Kuban, Odessa, Bessarabia), and is printed in the
Kievskaja Starina, May 1887, pp. 196-197:

"Long, long ago, when there was as yet in the world neither
people, nor earth, nor trees, nor birds, nor any kind of living
creature whatever, there was water everywhere; and above it
the first heaven, where lived God and his two servants, Mishka
and Grishka. . . . And in the same heaven where now is the
Mother of God, (since previously the first heaven has been mentioned, this must be the second). . . there lived Satanail, and
he did everything perverse to God. Whatever the Lord wanted
to do, Satanail would take it and mix it up, the wretch. And the
Lord began to think how to get rid of Satanail; but not to get
rid of him, but to take away his shirt, in which was Satanail's
power. Once Satanail undressed, put his shirt on a stone and
began to swim in the sea because the wretch liked to bathe; while
the Lord sits in his heaven and watches. And the Lord began to
tease Satanail. "You cannot," says he, "reach the bottom of the
sea." "Yes I can too," says the devil. And Satanail began to
try diving and the Lord called Michael and ordered him to fly
over the sea, and when Satanail dived, to blow on the sea.

"So it happened. Satanail dived the first time, and Mishka
began to blow on the water. Immediately the sea was covered
with a crust; it had frozen. Satanail rose up and broke the ice
with his head. The Lord says to him, "Dive," says he, "once
more!" They had an agreement to dive three times. Satanail
dived once more, and Mishka blows, and even sat down on the
water, he wanted so much to please God. The sea again became
covered with ice, even thicker. Satanail came out and again

broke the ice with his head. The Lord says to him, "Now dive the third time!" Satanail dived, and Mishka thought he would burst — he blows and blows on the water. And the Lord began to help him, he blows on the sea with all his strength. The sea became covered with such thick ice that Satanail, when he tried to come out, could not break through with his head, and in that time Grishka grabbed his shirt and started to lift himself to the sky. Satanail, when he saw that this business was not in fun, melted a hole and started after Grishka. He began to catch up, because Grishka had only two wings, and Satanail all of six. But luckily Mishka appears and cuts off Satanail's wings. Satanail fell into the sea, and Mishka and Grishka carried his shirt to God. It was in this same shirt that Jesus Christ was tortured on the cross; but the Lord made Mishka and Grishka the archangels Michael and Gabriel.

Veselovskij, in the oft-mentioned research into the legend of the dualistic world-creation, adduces another tale, set down in the article by Trusevič: Kosmogoničeskija predanija žitelej Poles'ja (Kiev and Volhynia), printed in Kievljanin 1866 #4. In this tale is told first how the angel dived to extract earth to create the dry land, then how the angel made for himself out of the hidden dirt hills and forests, how God created man, how the angel wished to do the same, how God cursed him and turned him into a devil. Finally is told how the Devil would not permit Adam to plow the land, saying that it was his, and how then he permitted him, after making Adam sign over to him all his children. This receipt the Devil hid in a stone and threw into the sea; but God plunged into the sea, took the receipt and returned it to Adam. Veselovskij sees in this tale "a union of the moment (the motif) of the diving at the world-creation with the moment of the second Bulgarian story: the receipt." We shall permit ourselves not to see here an influence from the tale lying in the base of the episode of the receipt in the Bulgarian legend, because in the Bulgarian legend it is not God but the Devil who dives (as in the Serbian and the two above-cited Ukrainian legends), while the Devil leaves Adam's bill on the shore (like the other objects which cause the struggle in the Serbian and the Ukrainian variants). It is obvious that the Devil's hiding the bill and God's taking it away from him are quite a different matter from the legends of seizing from the Devil, while he is diving, various objects that are precious to

him, among them the bill. This episode of the Polish variant
has developed simply out of the apocryphal tales in which the
Devil hides Adam's bill in the stone at the bottom of the river
Jordan. The power of this bill was broken by God's immersing
Christ above this stone. According to the Palestinian tales,
Christ had even to push the stone out onto the bank; for Deacon
Arsenius of Saloniki, in his travel to Jerusalem, observed: "An
on the bank of the Jordan a stone, with the footprints of Christ
on it, and under that stone the bones of a snake are seen; this
was the inscription of Adam."[15] According to other stories, it
is not the baptizing in the Jordan alone, but also the descent of
Christ into hell, that nullifies Adam's bill.[16]

It is much more to the point to notice the combination of the
two themes in the Bulgarian tales of the dualistic diving in the
following Ukrainian tale, inserted into Čubinskij: Trudy I: 35.

The whirlwind originated from that when Satanail extracted
earth from the water, the water froze on top. When Satanail
bumped through the ice he became very tired, but the angel was
already waiting for him above the ice, and grabbed away his
earth and flew to God. Satanail rested and started in pursuit.
God sees that Satanail will overtake the angel, and says to him,
"Make a sweep with your sword to the right." The angel made
the sweep and cut off the right wing of Satanail. The latter spun
around and (thus) became like a whirlwind. (That is why) even
now, when Satanail flies over the earth, immediately a whirlwind is raised. — We believe that this is a fragmentary tradition, poorly appropriated by the people, on the two above-cited
Ukrainian tales (the Novgorod-northern and the Kiev-an); a
tradition which in the beginning was assimilated with the theme,
very widespread in the Ukraine, but a peculiar one, of Satanail's
extracting dirt from the sea for God's sake. So that we do not
see in this fragment, either, any genetic connection with the
tales of Satanail's participation in the world-creation.

On reviewing all the Balkan and Ukraine variants of the tale
of wresting a precious object from Satan, we can conclude that
the tale on this theme has penetrated into the country of the
Balkan Slavs and of the Ukrainians, but without settling clearly
upon the object of dispute. That is why in one place it is called
"heavenly power", in other places a marvelous shirt, a crown,
the sun, a bill. This variety does away with the assumption
that they have all started from one written apocryphal narrative.

As for the various apocryphal details which these variants share
with such monuments, such as the Liber S. Johannis, the Discourse of the Three Prelates et al. (a number of heavens, the
transformation of the crown into the sun, God's shirts, etc.),
they could have entered into them later.[17] In its texture and in
the antiquity of its cosmographic details, which recall Hither-
Asiatic cosmogonies (double heavens, the conquering of the
second heaven by Satanail, the obstacles to God's creating), the
variant in Kievskaja Starina is especially distinctive. Therefore
we consider it to be older than the Balkan tales. This variant
recalls by its character the cosmogonic tales of Irano-Chaldea,
the Mandean and the Yezid. All of this does away with the assumption that the Ukrainian variants are settlers from out of
the Balkans along with the written apocryphas. They must have
come by some straighter route from Asiatic country, where
various Gnostic cosmogonies were formed. But by what kind
of medium? This is still impossible to answer.

For the present we consider it possible to bring together
the basis of these tales with the notions that we find in some
sacred Iranian books and which are set forth in Darmsteter:
Etudes iraniennes II: 225-229. According to the Iranian notions,
because of his sin there flew away from Yima Kshaet (Jemshid)
his holy power (hvarenô) — three lights; which power was seized
by the demon Franhacyan (Afrasiab). In protecting his new ac-
quisition, among other things he dives three times into the sea;
but Haoma catches up with him and binds him, and takes away
from him his heavenly power.

We have no intention now of letting ourselves compose any
closer and more definite account of how this Iranian imagery
could have passed westward and developed into those images
which we have just seen in the Ukrainian tales, in the Serbian
and the Bulgarian; but at all events we insist that these legends
in their plot have nothing in common with the tales of the diving
by Satan into the primeval sea after particles of dirt out of which
God creates dry land.

Thus, in all the oral literature of the Balkan Slavs, which
already has been explored considerably (although much is still to
be desired in the investigation of the Serbian folk prose), up to
now only one rather short Bulgarian tale is known on this
theme. And this speaks but poorly in favor of the assumption that this tale has developed out of written Bogomil

apocryphas, which once spread so fervently throughout the Balkan peoples.

In the country of the Austrian Slavs, the close kin of the Serbs, up to the present only one tale has been recorded which can be admitted as an echo of the Bulgarian tale. This is the Slovene legend inserted by Erben into Časopis Českého Muzea, and reprinted by Kreck in Einleitung in die slavische Literatur-geschichte, 783.

In the beginning there was nothing but God. He slept and dreamt, and the dream lasted for centuries. And it was destined that he should awake. He awoke and God began to look around, and wherever he looked a star appeared. And the Lord began to wonder at this that his eye had done. And he went and went, but nowhere was there a beginning or an end; he saw under him only the sea. He stepped into the sea and dived clear to its bottom. When he came up again, under one of his nails there had lodged a grain of sand. The grain of sand fell and floated on the water, and this grain of sand is our earth, and the depth of the sea is its native home.

In this tale the original base has been so weakened that the dualism has actually disappeared: God himself plunges into the sea to extract a grain of sand. According to ethnographic re-lationships, this tale should have had to pass to the Slovenes through Serbia; but the entry could also have been gained by some other route, one not even through the Balkan peninsula.

Notes

1. For the Armenian Paulician sects of Asia Minor and the connection of the Bogomils with them, see Döllinger: Beiträg zur Sectengeschichte des Mittelalters. Geschichte der gnostisch manichäischen Secten im früheren Mittelalter. 1890.

2. The most detailed history and survey of the Bogomil beliefs is that of Rački, in Bogomili i Patereni (Rad Jugoslavens. akademije znanosti i umjetnosti, kn. VII, VIII, X). Noteworthy among recent surveys are Jireček: Istorija Bolgar" and Pypin: Istorija slavjanskix" literatur" I.

3. These two persons can be merged into one; since, ac-cording to the teaching of many Gnostics and Bogomils, the son of God is one and the same person as the angel Michael. Farthe on we shall see that in a Ukrainian (Chernigov) variant of the

fight between the angel and the Devil, the former is called Michael.

4. It is inserted also in Migne: "Patrologiae cursus completus. Series graeca. v. 128. Panoplia dogmatica, tit. XXVII."

5. Šapkarevə: Bəlg. nar. prik. i věrv. 9-10. For the French translation and our notes to it, see Mélusine 1888 #12. Cf. Veselovskij: Razyskanija, VI-X: 328-332, 458-459. For a similar tale see Čubinskij: Trudy eksped. I: 145.
It may be thought that these stories arose out of the creation of the wolf by Ahriman as the counter to the creation of the dog by Ormuzd (Vendidad XIII: 1, 113-114; Spiegel: Avesta I: 197; Eranische Altertumskunde II: 145 etc.; but in their present form these tales are strongly altered with respect to the ancient Iranian — if indeed they arose from them.

6. We have selected out the more characteristic expressions from the writings of Thilo and of Döllinger.

7. It is interesting to compare this detail with the detail of the burning sand which scorched the Devil in the Gypsy tail related above.

8. Cf. again the corresponding detail in the Gypsy variant.

9. The conceit of the waters above the sky (celestial ocean) belongs to Chaldean cosmography, and from the latter it passed to the Hebrews. See Jensen: Die Kosmologie der Babilonier (Strassburg 1890), where at the end is added a picture of the world according to Babylonian conceptions; it is interesting from the standpoint of mediaeval cosmographic ideas.

10. See the end of Ch. V.

11. Since Russian has no definite article, this may be translated, indifferently, "I am a God." EWC

12. Latinization of the Russian ours. — EWC

13. Porfirjev" (Apokr. skaz. o vetxozav. licax" etc.: Sobyt. po rukop. Solov. bibl., 31) says that the detail (in the "Svitok") of the diver is a substitution from "the national mythical tales", but he does not specify from which ones.

14. I.e., one out of glass-crystal.

15. Porfirjev": Apokrifič. skaz. o vetxozavětnyx" licax" i sobytijax", 178.

16. In Tixonravov, Pamjatniki otrečennoj literatury I: 16-17.
The holy apostle Bartholomew questions the holy apostle Andrew
the First-Called as to how and in what image our forefather Cain
was born and how our forefather Adam gave his inscription to
the Devil. Our forefather Cain was born filthy; although his
head was like unto that of other men, on his chest and his forehead there were twelve heads of snakes (cf. Tsogak in the Shah-
Nameh); thus it was that whenever Eve fed him from her breasts
then the snakes' heads tore at her vitals, and from this tearing
and dire torment our foremother Eve became scabby. And Adam
saw his wife suffering greatly, and he sorrowed over her. And
there came to him the Devil in the form of a man and said unto
him: "What wilt thou give to me, that I should heal thy son Cain
and rescue thy wife Eve from such torment?" And Adam spake
to him: "And what should I give thee?" And the Devil said, "Give
me thine inscription." And Adam said unto him, "What kind of
inscription should I give thee?" And the Devil spake: "Do thou
slay a kid and write down upon a stone that I shall give thee, and
say thereby, 'The living to God, the dead to thee.'" And Adam
did as the Devil had commanded him, and he brought to him a
great slab of stone, and Adam slew a kid, and drew forth the
blood in a vessel, and wet both hands upon the slab of white stone
and the hands of Adam were imprinted on this slab. And the
Devil went to Cain and plucked the twelve heads of snakes; he
placed them upon the stone and upon the inscription and cast it
all into the river Jordan and commanded the heads of the snakes
to guard this inscription, and it was under the ward of those
snakes's heads until the coming of our Lord Jesus Christ. And
when he came to the Jordan to be baptized for the sake of our
salvation, then did the heads of the snakes arise in the waves of
the Jordan against the Lord and he crushed the heads of the
snakes in the water. And the Devil saw the heads of the snakes
crushed; and then the Devil took the remains of this inscription
to hell, where also were the saints shut in. When our Lord
Jesus Christ rose from the dead, at that time he wiped out the
remains of Adam's inscription and smoothed it over and bound
the Devil; and he freed the souls from hell . . . and led them
unto paradise to his Father and his domain." Cf. ibid. 12-13,
301.

We have inserted the lengthy extract also for the purpose
of letting the reader compare it with the Bulgarian and the Trans-
Caucasian tales, indicated above, of the agreement between God
and Satan which was destroyed by Christ.

The snakes with human heads at the feet of Christ at his
baptism are shown in the drawings of the baptism (see Didron:
Iconographie Chrétienne, Histoire de Dieu, 578). For the bibliography of the apocryphas in which Adam's bill is mentioned,
see above and also Ch. V.

17. Let us remark that although we do not agree with the general explanation of these tales offered by Veselovskij, we appreciate none the less the approximations of particular and various details to those of the written apocryphas.

5 The widespread occurrence of the legends of the dualistic cosmogony among the Russian Slavs. — The Ukrainian Christmas carols about the creator-doves and about God and the two apostles; their independent character, distinct from the prose tales; probability of a southeastern Gnostic and Iranian influence upon the Russian center, and traces of it. — The Ukrainian prose variants of the tale of the dualistic cosmogony; their dissimilarity to the Bulgarian tale and their resemblance to the northeastern, the Finno-Turkic and the Altai-Mongolian. — The question of borrowing. — The greater probablity of movement of the cosmogonic tale from the east to Russia than vice versa: the original and ancient traits in the Mordvin, Yenissei-Turkic, and Altai-Mongolian variants. — The northern cosmogonic tales: the Vogul, Buryat, Yakut: their hybrid character. — The feeble echoes of the Russian variants of the dualistic cosmogony among the Slovaks, Poles, Lithuanians. — The Rumanian variant. — Comparative notes on the Bulgarian tale from Obšt Trud. — The episode of the billy-goat and the calf. — Adam's bill. — Conception from a flower. — Birth of Jesus. — Jordan. — Judas.

When we pass from the country of the Balkan Slavs to that of the Russian, we shall be struck squarely by the great plenty of legends about the dualistic world-creation among the latter. Out of the variants collected in Veselovskij's works a whole little volume could be made; and since his investigation new ones have been printed in Etnografičeskoe Obozrenie XIII-XIV: 68-74, 250-252; XV: 190-191, (the beginning of the last legend is the narrative of the Tiberian sea, transmitted orally). Beside this, we must add here two more White-Russian variants, printed in vol. IV of Romanov's Belorusskij Sbornik. It is a little hard for us to imagine that the Balkan poverty could have given rise to such a wealth. We would sooner allow that the episode of the Devil's diving into the sea in the Bulgarian dualistic tale has been carried in a weakened form to Bulgaria from Russia, than the reverse. Aside from this, there are other reasons for believing that the Russian variants of the dualistic world-creation

have been composed independently of Balkan — in this case
Bulgarian — influence.

Among the Ukrainian variants, the Christmas carols which
we adduced at the beginning of this work draw our attention first
of all. These Christmas carols differ from the prose tales in
that they do not mention the name of Satanail. In the one, the
co-workers of God in extracting sand from the bottom of the
sea for "sowing the world," are identified as Sts. Peter and
Paul; although their attempt fails, so that God himself plunges
into the sea after they do. It is hard for us to imagine that this
Christmas carol is simple and at the same time the later reworking of the prose tale of Satanail and God. This tale, we shall
notice, in the Ukraine has a humorous character: Satanail is
presented in a ridiculous light. It is impossible to substitute
saints for the despised and comical Satanail, and two of them at
that. The Christmas carol must be older than the prose tales:
in favor of this is its verse form of an ancient ceremonial song,
which has been taken down in but one variant; hence it is forgotten as a rare antique, while the prose tales of Satanail continue to spread.

In the other Christmas carol are represented three divine
birds, perched upon a tree in the primeval sea, taking counsel
on how to obtain sand and a golden stone from the bottom of the
sea, that they may create from them the earth and the heaven
with its lights.[1] This Christmas carol must be much the older,
by virtue of its bird-form and the anonymity of the demiurges.
We have already had occasion to indicate its kinship with the
cosmogonic tales of the Yezids and the Irano-Chaldean notions
of the world-tree. . . . This Christmas carol carries us into a
circle of ideas like those of the Zervanites or certain Gnostics,
according to which the primeval God appears in the beginning
with two sons who later shall be mutual antagonists: Ormuzd
and Ahriman, Word-Christ and Satanail, Michael (or Gabriel)
and Satan, etc.[2] In the popular reworking of such notions, and
the more in places far removed from the site of the more literary theosophic origin of these notions, these personages easily
could lose their names, or else receive the names of apostles
as popularized by the Christian church, just as among the Yezids
the ancient names of the Iranian demiurges were replaced with
names of Judeo-Moslem angels and saints.[3]

Just as neither in the folk literature of the Balkan Slavs nor their apocryphas are there images similar to those which are in the base of the above-cited Ukrainian Christmas carols, so there is no justification for assuming that these songs have inevitably been compounded under the influence of Balkan ideas. They must have been compounded, or at least they could have been compounded, under the influence of that current of religious ideas which has traveled to Europe out of Hither Asia, and which generated the Balkan heresies themselves, alongside of the other spiritual phenomena of that nature. And that current could have flowed into Russia not only via the Balkan peninsula, through which indeed there have passed to Russia many Hither-Asiatic ideas along with the Bulgarian apocryphas, but also by a straighter route through the Asia Minor-Caucasian country; and beside this, also from the southeast, via sundry Turkic tribes which were subjected to the same influence from Iran.

On the whole we are very much inclined to derive all the influence of Judeo-Christian and apocryphal ideas in Russia through that southwestern route by which there came here the official form of Christianity and literature. Along with this there are indications also of a cross-influence on Russian soil, for instance an Iranian; and this earlier than the ecclesiastical or Bulgarian apocryphal propaganda. Thus, e.g., as early as 1071 there is recorded in a Russian chronicle (in the transcript of Lavrentij) the appearance of magi near Belozer, who said: "We know how man was created: God was washing in the bathhouse and, after sweating, he wiped himself with a towel that he threw onto the ground; then Satan entered into dispute with God as to who should make man out of this towel; and God breathed a soul into him, therefore after death man's body returns to the soil, and his spirit to God." Whether these magi were of a Finnic tribe or a Russian is immaterial; but it is curious that the idea they expounded should resemble the Mandean and the other apocryphal cosmogonies; while the idea of God's sweat, which was used as an element in the creation of the first man, is found in the Bundahish. There it tells actually that Ormuzd created from his sweat or from the matter sucked out of the sweat, the primeval man (the Proto-Adam of the Gnostics), whom later Ahriman did to death (Iusti: Der Bundehesch, 6, ch. 3, X, 12; Darmsteter, op.cit., 137). Obviously, such ideas could have been carried up the Volga, into the present-day northern Great-Russian country, and earlier than they penetrated Christianity; certainly at least before the supremacy of the latter became established.[4]

This is one of the few definitely known indications of the ancient Irano-Chaldean influence in the Russian country, which was not altogether weak during the period of the Sassanian kingdom, and which on the one hand touched upon the country of the Central Asiatic Turanians and on the other had relationships with those people north of the Caucasus whom the Armenian writers call Huns (Elisée Vartabed: Soulèvement national de l'Arménie chrétienne au V-e siècle contre la loi de Zoroastre, 90-91, 111). The religious influence of Iran upon the Trans-Caucasian tribes is known. It would be strange if it did not traverse the Caucasian forests; all the more since even to this day there survives there the Iranian tribe of Ossetes, whose colonies existed formerly in various places in southern Russia.[5] On the ground of the above-cited detail from the Yezid tradition that the supreme deity sits upon a thorn, we have already recalled the detail in a Ukrainian tradition of the creation of the first people, according to which God first of all created a wife for Adam out of a bouquet of roses and, when Adam demurred at taking such a wife, God said that he would keep her as the mother of his son (Čubinskij; Trudy I: 145-146). Veselovskij, in analyzing this legend in his academic treatise (p. 13ff), says: "The tradition of the creation of woman from a flower belongs to the small circle of tales the source of which must be sought in some Christian apocrypha." Up to the present, no such apocrypha is known; at any event, it does not occur in the Slavic literature. Moreover, the first-created woman, who became the mother of God's son, reminds us of the Gnostic ideas about Jesus Christ as the Proto-Adam and about Mary as the Proto-Eve, while at the same time the body of this woman from a rose reminds us of how the wise Yezid god obtained his primeval or his first-born son (Proto-Adam, Michael, Jesus) from the thorn on a branch.[6]

Such now are the fragmentary data on the influence of Irano-Chaldean beliefs upon the Russian country, independent of the mediacy of the Balkan peoples. Why should there not also have formed, independently of this medium, the above-cited Christmas carols?

When we turn to the numerous Ukrainian variants of the prose tale about Satanail extracting lumps of dirt from the bottom of the sea at God's command, we need stop only over some of their details, for the common character of these and the Bulgarian shows up from the variant we printed at the beginning of this investigation of ours.

First of all we shall remark that of the Ukrainian variants to this tale there are many in print (more than 12), and they are almost all more widespread than the corresponding Bulgarian episode in the tale "Obšt Trud." One of the characteristic differences is that in the Bulgarian tale there is not at all the detail of the mountains being formed from lumps of dirt which Satanail hid in his mouth; a detail which we see in almost all Russian and Finno-Turkic variants. Furthermore, many of the Ukrainian variants contain cosmogonic details of a more ancient character than those given us by the Bulgarian episode. Thus, one of the variants in Čubinskij (I: 143-144) is introduced thus: "In the beginning there was neither earth nor heaven; there was only darkness and water mixed with earth, and God flew over the water, which bubbled like foam." (Cf. p. 191: "When the heaven was ready, but there still was no earth, but only water in the form of froth, Satan Lucifer howled in this froth.") This froth corresponds in the very beginning to the condensed water of the Chaldean cosmogonies and to the froth of which it is said in the Discourse of the Three Prelates that "the Lord commanded that the sea foam be gathered and that the land be made," etc. Similar differences of the Ukrainian variants from the Bulgarian demonstrate the independent borrowing of their distribution, in which the Ukrainian type has received some roaming imagery from the ancient cosmogonies. The other Ukrainian variants contain details that they hold in common with some Finno-Turkic variants. Thus, in the Galician variant, printed by Erben in Sto prostonárodnich poh. a pov. nár., 143-144, God is sailing over the sea in a boat when he meets the Devil, who is lying in the foam while in the Kharkov variant the Lord Savaoth is astride an ark (Etnografičeskoe Obozrenie XIII-XIV: 69). In this, of course, a written influence shows through; but the idea that even God must have a support on the water, is met also in a Mordvin variant, where God is floating on a stone; and in a Turco-Altaian, where God and the Devil are also sitting on a rock.[7]

In the White-Russian variants, the beginning is interesting, where God meets a bladder floating on the water, and the Devil comes out of it. This bladder recalls the egg in the Asiatic cosmogonies.

The Great-Russian variants, which are considerable in number (about ten have been printed), may be divided into two kinds: "scholarly" (probably from the Raskolniks), and "common." The former are replete with details which sometimes are of bookish character, so that they even approach the written "Bundle of Divine Books" (e.g., the variant of Rybnikov); while others obviously developed in most recent times, with new details, although their style is archaic (the variants of E. Barsov and Derunov). The other group confuses Biblical events and personages (e.g., Noah the Just in Afanasiev's version) and atrophy the basic motives; while they lay special stress upon the quarrel between God and Satan over seniority and title (variant of Jakuškin). Among the details of some Great-Russian variants, special attention is deserved by the notion of the two demiurges, God and Satan, in the form of birds, swans (which do not occur in the northern part of Russia), similar to the notion of the Finno-Turkic variants (among the Cheremiss, Keremet [Satan] is in the form of a duck; among the Mordvins Shaitan is in the form of a bird; among the Altaians, both gods are swans).

Such similarities of many Russian variants — Great-Russian and Ukrainian — with the Finno-Turkic, raise the question all the more: Who took the tale from whom — the Russians from the "aboriginals" or vice versa? The notion of the demiurges, or at least one of them, in the form of a bird, speaks rather in favor of the opinion that the tale has been carried from the aboriginals to the Russians rather than the reverse. Had the reverse been the case, the variants of this tale should have moved from southwest to northeast, from Ukraine to Siberia. But the Ukrainian as well as the White-Russian variants are completely anthropomorphic, whereas almost all the aboriginal variants are ornithomorphic; while the Great-Russian occupy an intermediate position between them. It is much more natural to allow that the character of the mythology has been heightened, rather than that it has fallen as the variants passed from one people to another.

Moreover, many of the aboriginal variants contain special details, and they are of popular, archaic nature, such as are not found in the Russian variants. For instance, in the Mordvin variants, on the whole makedly more integrated than many of the lowly Great-Russian variants (e.g., of Jakuškin, Afanasiev), Shaitan proceeds from God's spittle, as the angel in the Trans-Caucasian variants does from his tear, etc. (vide supra). There again we see also an agreement between the two gods, and not between Adam and Shaitan; as would have been the case had this detail been taken from the Slavo-Russian apocrypha. In the Altaian tales, which on the whole are more developed than the Russian, we have already pointed to details such as are absent from the Russian variants and which occur in the ancient Asiatic cosmogonies. We shall add to what has been said, that the agreement between the deities bears no resemblance to the bill which Adam gave to Satan; and it is not a mere agreement between two deities, but an agreement that the Devil Erlik shall not bear hostility against God, nor do mischief to the people; i.e., an agreement which recalls the truce between Ormuzd and Ahriman. Although farther on, in the other variant, the dead belong to Erlik, it does not say that this dominion has been taken from him, as in the Christian apocryphas; which means that Erlik appears as the recognized king of the earth's womb, something like Hades. In the same variant (Potanin's) Erlik appears as more significant than the god Ülgen: it is he, and not Ülgen, who animates man. It is this way also in the new variant where a third god appears, who accomplishes what in the Bulgarian and the Ukrainian tales is done by Satanail; i.e., he enlarges the earth by carrying the two sleeping gods.

On the whole, in the Yeniseian and Altaian variants, as in the Turkic, as well as the Mongolian, the devil appears as more knowing and powerful[8] than even in the Trans-Caucasian and the Bulgarian variants; to say nothing of the Russian, where the Devil plays a subordinate and even comic role. So that if the opinion were to be accepted that the Central Asiatic variants are reflections of the Bogomil, we should have to say that the Yeniseian-Altaian disciples of the Russians had turned out plus bogoumiles que les bogoumiles eux-mêmes; for in the majority of the Bogomil variants and in the Book of John itself, the dualism is softened and the Devil is subordinate to God. All these circumstances speak in favor of the hypothesis that the bases of our dualistic tale were constituted in Irano-Chaldean country, and that from there they have spread on the one hand in a weakened form out of the Caucasus, thence into Bulgaria; and on the other into Central Asia, where they have been preserved most fully; to travel thence into Russia likewise in a comparatively weakened form.[9]

In this investigation of ours we have no reason to pay much attention to the most northerly Uralo-Siberian variants of the tale of the Devil's obtaining earth from the sea-bottom. These variants are set forth in considerable detail by Veselovskij; so that we shall merely point in addition to the Vogul legend adduced by Lucien Adam: Une genèse Wogule, in Revue de Philologie et d'Ethnographie I (1874); (Paris, publ. par M. de Ujfalvy); and reproduced by H. de Charencey: Une légende cosmogonique (Havre 1884); further, the Buryat variant of the creations of man and dog, adduced in the article by Schiefner: Zur vergleichenden Thiersagenkunde, in Inland #3 (1862). After that we shall cast only a fleeting glance at these northern tales, for the sake of elucidating the common opinion as to the place they occupy in the evolution of the known dualistic tales of the world-creation. These tales, in our opinion, contain echoes of the Turkic and Altaio-Mongolian dualistic legends, but now with the dualism weakened, and containing an admixture of native tales which in part recall the American; plus Christian nomenclature actually taken from the Russians.

Among the Voguls we find one of the gods diving for earth, in the form or the dress of a bird, but without any antagonism between the gods, and only after the older god had made a dwelling for the first of a pair of people, although it was a cramped one. Moreover, the demiurge is represented as the son of this pair. In the legend belonging to the Manzi, who are the kin of the Voguls, two birds appear, of which one extracts earth from the sea, while the other attempts to do the same, but without success, falls down as though dead, and is resuscitated by the first bird. Among the Buryats, the tall, spare, white man, without any antagonism toward God, dives at his command, extracts clay from the sea-bottom and himself sows it over the surface of the sea. Among the Yakuts, in some tales there is no diving, but God creates the world and the Devil spoils it with mountains, valleys, and rivers; or he spoils it again, like Ahriman in the Bundahish. The cross-influence of the Iranian ideas upon the Yakuts will surprise no one; sufficient to recall that this people is a Turkic tribe and has lived formerly farther southwest from its present habitations. In another Yakut legend there is the diving of two birds (similar to the legend of the Manzi and those of the Americans); but here they bring upon the scene Jesus Christ, the Mother of God, Nicholas the Thaumaturge and seven angels; while the arranger of the creation is the Mother of God. It were interesting to continue the investigation into the Yakut legend, in order to see how much native mythology is hidden under the Christian nomenclature.

There remains for us to cast our glance toward the western neighbors of the Russian Slavs. Here we find throughout only muffled echoes of our dualistic tale. Thus, among the Slovaks we find only a tale about the origin of the mountains: God carried dirt in a kerchief and sowed it, while the Devil chased after him and poked a hole through the kerchief; this caused an uneven outpour — the Tatras. However, we cannot be confident in asserting that this Slovak legend has derived from the Russian dualistic tale; for, among the Bulgarians, in whose dualistic tale there is no creation of the mountains by the devil, we find the same belief that "The Old Lord was carrying a bag of flour, and the bag was torn, so that wherever the flour poured out there the hills and mountains were formed" (Sbornik za narodno umotvorenie V: iii: 109). Among the Poles there is the same notion, according to which God had first created the earth flat, but the Devil taught the duck to steal a little earth; God, on seeing this, sent after it a hawk; as soon as the hawk scented the duck, the latter dropped the dirt, and this is what made the mountains. Another Polish legend has retained from the Russian tale only the detail that God created the earth from a grain of sand, which he placed upon a cross made of two fishes.

The Lithuanian legend has taken over more from the Russian tale; according to it, the devil dives for dirt at God's command; but he takes the dirt not only in his mouth or his hands but also in his ears, nose, eyes, etc.

Obviously, the Catholic clerical influence has halted the spread of the dualistic legends to the west of the Russian country.

Veselovskij adduces from Fr. Müller's book, Siebenbürgisch Sagen (p. 162) the content of a Roumanian cosmogonic legend, remarking quite correctly that it is not distinguished for its degree of conservatism: "In the beginning of the world there was only water. God sent the archangel Gabriel to bring sand from the sea-bottom, but it fell through his hands, so that there remained but a few grains under his nails, and from them God made the earth. It stretched away evenly over the water, like layer-bread but the hedgehog spoke up from the bushes that it should be thicker. So God made it that way." (Veselovskij, Razyskanija

XI-XVII: 364). Sârcu informed Veselovskij that the dualistic
tale of the world-creation is known also among the Bessarabian
Roumanians; here the Devil appears as God's antagonist. It
would be very desirable to have such a tale in print. For the
present it is very hard to make any decisive judgment about the
Transylvanian tale, in virtue of its fragmentary nature. But its
very fragmentary nature testifies that it is at a distance from
the focus of these tales in Europe. This tale is more analogous
to the Ukrainian Christmas carol of the diving by the apostles
than to the Bulgarian tale of the Devil's diving; therefore it can
hardly be counted as an echo of the Bulgarian legend.

The Bulgarian tale printed in Obšt Trud contains many details which are interesting for the comparative investigation of
religious traditions; but most of these details go beyond the
limits of our investigation. Therefore we shall confine ourselves
here to setting forth, with a few additions, our notes to the French
translation of this tale, which was published in Mélusine #10
(1888). This publication is but poorly known in Bulgaria.

The episode of the goat and the bee. This entire part of the
legend bears even more than what goes before the imprint of
ideas akin to the Syrian Gnosticism (Marcion, the Ophites) and
the Iranian (Manicheanism). The Lord (the God of the Old Testament) is represented here as weaker than the Devil: he cannot
stop the increase in size of the earth, so he turns for counsel
to the Devil, who here takes the place of the supreme deity. This
detail is analogous with the episode in the Ukrainian tale where
the growth of the mountains which proceeded from the Devil's
mouth is stopped only by the Apostles Paul and Peter and not
by God (Dragomanov, Malorusk. nar. predanija i raskazy, p. 90).
The goat is a creation of the Devil, also according to the Ukrainian beliefs (Čubinskij: Trudy I: 49), the White Russian (Romanov:
Belorusskij Sbornik IV: 2), the Great-Russian (Sadovnikov:
Narodnyja skazki Samarskago kraja p. 251), the Lithuanian
(Etnografičeskoe Obozrenie VI: 140), the German (Grimm:
Haus- und Kindermärchen #148), the Votyak (Veselovskij:
Razyskanija XI-XVII: 367-368), etc. In the Moslem tradi-
tions, the angel of death comes to Adam in the form of a
buck-goat (Weil: Biblische Legenden der Musulmänner, 42).
As we have already noticed, similar notions can be traced
back to the Assyro-Chaldean ideas: in them the goat appears
as the enemy of the vineyard, which often is identified with

the tree of life (Lenormant: Les origines de l'histoire 75-
83. . .)

There were churchly-Christian reasons, readily understand-
able, and also still older ones, why the bee had to be represented as a sacred animal. In a Serbian legend (Krauss: Sagen und
Märchen der Südslaven II: 422), the bee was produced from the
wound which an evil woman inflicted upon Christ. This belief
recalls the Indian representation of Krishna, whose legend has
much in common with that of Christ, with a bee on his forehead
(De Gubernatis: Mythologie Zoologique II: 288), and the Greek
belief that Dionysius when killed in the form of a bull returns
to life as a bee (ibid.). According to the beliefs of the Chuvash
and the Russians in the Kazan government, the bee originated
from the navel of the great god, or of Christ through his suffering. (Magnitskij: Materialy v ob'jasnenju staroj čuvašskoj very
251: in Veselovskij: Razyskanija XI: 96). The detail of the bee
in the Bulgarian tale can be placed beside the Caucasian belief
that the bees are the only animals God created in paradise (De
Gubernatis, ibid., 229, 230, where a German gloss is adduced
that "the nobility of the bee has come from paradise"). The
Ukrainian notion that St. Zosimus (along with St. Sabbatius, the
patron of the bees among the Russians) brought the bees out of
"the place of the idols" or, according to other tradition, "from
the mountain," seems to us a distortion of a similar Caucasian
notion. However, in the Ukraine and in White-Russia there is
another kind of belief about the bee: that it is evil, that it even
tries to deceive God (Dragomanov, op. cit., 1-2, Das Ausland
#50 (1870)). According to Magyar beliefs, the bee likewise is
at one time evil, at another it is a creation by God (H. v.
Wlisłoski, Volksglaube und religiöser Brauch der Magyaren,
94-95).

In Bulgaria there is recorded a variant different from the
episode given above about the service which the bee rendered
God: "When the Lord made the heaven and earth, he made the
earth larger; so that the heaven could not cover it. The Lord
saw that the Devil was talking about something with the hedgehog, so he sent the bee to listen to what was being said. 'The
Lord does not know,' the Devil was saying to the hedgehog, 'that
he should take a stick and poke and poke the earth, to make
valleys, hilltops; then the earth will be smaller, and the heaven
will be able to cover it.' When the bee heard this, it went and

reported to the Lord. So the Lord made the valleys and heights
of the earth, so that the heaven covered it; and then he blessed
the bee: its spittle should serve for a candle at baptisms and
weddings, and its hive for prayer." (Sborn. za nar. umotv.
IV: iii: 129. Similar to this, without the Devil and the bee —
ibid., I: 105). Cf. the Ukrainian Christmas carol above, on the
quarrel between the Lord and Peter, where the earth is the
larger because it is not even.

Adam's bill. In Bulgaria there is recorded still another
variant of the agreement with the Devil, which is closer to the
tale of the written Slavic apocryphas: Sborn. za nar. umotvor.
VI: iii: 113. After his expulsion from paradise, Adam plows
the land; the Devil forbids him, and finally says to him: "The
means for your living, this I will give to you, when you give me
a bill for your offspring that will be born to you: that the living
be yours and the dead mine." He and his wife thought it over,
they talked it over, they agreed, and Adam gave him a bill from
his hand, written on a slab with blood from the body of Adam.
The Devil took the slab and he hid it down below under the cauldron in hell. It stayed there, and all the people who died, all
of them went into the cauldron of eternal torment, until Christ
went to the eternal torment and broke up the slab which Adam
had given in place of a bill." (Cf. Tixonravov: Pamjatniki
otreč. russkoj literatury I: 12).

In Etnografičeskoe Obozrenie XIII-XIV: 74-76 there are recorded from the Kharkov government some oral Ukrainian tales
of Adam's bill, which are very close to the written apocryphas.
In one of them it is said that the stone with Adam's inscription
came out of the Jordan of itself, after the baptism of the "thrice
born man," i.e., Jesus Christ.

For the bibliography of the narratives concerning Adam's
inscription, see above.

The evolution of the narratives about Adam's inscription
presents itself in this manner: First stage: An agreement between Ormuzd and Ahriman for lordship over the world in periods, in the Iranian monuments (Bundahish I, see above;
Minokhired in Spiegel: Die traditionelle Literatur der Persen,
95-98, 143); Second stage: Agreements between Satanail and
God that man shall belong to the two of them (among the Bogomils); Third stage: agreement between Satanail and God for di-
viding the dominion over the earth and the heaven, over the dead

and the living (in the oral tales of the Finno-Turks, Trans-Caucasians, and the two Bulgarian tales in Obšt Trud and Period Spis., see above); Fourth stage: Agreement between the Devil and Adam for the same: in the Slavic-Russian apocryphas, the Russian folk tales and the Bulgarian adduced above. But even in these stories the link with the preceding stage has been kept: the Devil does not permit Adam to plow the land, persuading him that only paradise and heaven are God's, while the earth belongs to him, the Devil.

The narrative adduced in Tixonravov'' under title, "Birth of Cain and inscription of Adam," in the matter of the inscription stands isolated from all the above-cited cases.

Conception from a flower. Impregnation from a flower is one of the most widely-spread notions in the folklore of various peoples. In Europe we find it as far back as the classic myth of Mars born of Juno (Ovid: Fasti V: 253 seq.). Among the eastern traditions, many of the gods' adventures come about by way of fruits; but there are even instances of conception from a flower (Benfey, in Götting. gelehrte Anzeigen (1858): 1511). This is the way Christian apocryphas explain the birth of many saints. In the French poetry of the XII century (Histoire littérai de la France XVII: 834-836), Abraham's daughter conceives from the odor of a flower on the tree of life and bears Fanuel, who conceives in her knee by the sap of this tree Anna the mother of Mary. Another apocryphal Old French poem, "Sur la conception records that St. Ann conceived from a flower. Veselovskij has already put these French poems beside the episode in our Bulgarian tale (Razyskanija X: 418-423, Žurn. Min. Nar. Prosv. March 1888: 245. Bonnard: Les traductions de la Bible en vers français au Moyen âge, 181. Chanbaneau: Les romans de saint Fenuel, in Revue des langues romanes, Sept.-Déc. 1885). A mediaeval tradition derives the conceiving of Jesus Christ himself from the odor of a flower (Keller: Li romans des sept sages CXCVIII).

This theme is widespread in many folk tales and songs. Thu in Pentamerone 18; in Schott: Walachische Märchen: Florianu, later in de Charencey: Le fils de la vierge; Id., Les traditions relatives au fils de la vierge. We have ourselves surveyed many Bulgarian and other similar tales in the article on Roždenieto na Konstantina Veliki.[10]

A notion similar to that found in the Bulgarian tale, how Mary conceived from the odor of a flower, is encountered in the Moslem traditions in which Mary conceives because the angel Gabriel breathed into her chest (Weil: Biblische Legenden der Musulmänner, 284). Many churchly writers, like Augustine, Ephraem et al., affirmed that Mary conceived through her ear (Virgo per aurem impregnabatur), and this belief is shared by the Meronites to this day (A. Maury, Essai sur les légendes pieuses du Moyen âge 179-180). So the Bogomils thought too (Thilo: Codex apocryphicus N. Testamenti 838).

The birth of Jesus. The miraculous emergence of Jesus through his mother's chest in a Bulgarian tale has a likeness to the Ukrainian tale where Jesus came forth from his mother's head, after the Holy Spirit had entered into her mouth (Čubinskij: Trudy I: 152). In the Mandean traditions, John the Baptist and Jesus were born this way (Siouffi: Etudes sur la religion des Soubbas, 4-6, 136-137). According to the statement of A. Lang, such a thing is said in an Irish ancient Christian legend which is still unpublished (Lang: Myth, Ritual and Religion I: 133, note). According to Buddhist traditions, Buddha came forth from his mother's bosom through her flank (Lalita Vistara, trad. de Foucaux, 77; Koeppen: Religion des Buddha I: 76, 77). The Christians had long known this tradition in a stronger guise; for Hieronimus said that "according to the Indian gymnosophists, Buddha was born of a virgin through her flank" (Rhys Davids: Buddhism, 183, note 1). However, such opinions are widespread even among primitive peoples (Waitz: Anthropologie der Naturvölker IV: 141-143; de Charencey, op. cit.).

Jordan. The brother of Mary, Jordan, is of course John the Baptist. The eastern traditions have always held him out as a close relative of Mary. Already in the Gospel of Luke (I: 36), Elizabeth, John's mother, is called a relative of Mary. The apocryphal Proto-evangelion calls John a cousin of Mary (Brunet: Les évangiles apocryphes 122, ch. XI). According to the Mandean traditions, Miriam the mother of Jesus and Enochuei John's mother were sisters (Siouffi, l. c.). The episode in the Bulgarian tale of John's attempt on the life of Mary still awaits clarification through investigation of the eastern Messianic legends.

Judas. As a point of departure for the legends of Judas similar to the episode in the Bulgarian tale, there may have served the alteration of the notions of those Gnostics who were called

Cainites and Judaites, and who revered Judas as a conscious contriver of man's redemption through Jesus' suffering (Matter: Histoire critique du gnosticisme II: 255; Migne: Dictionnaire des apocryphes II: 449). The episode of Judas in the Bulgarian tale is met in the Coptic legend placed among the apocryphal deeds of Sts. Andrew and Paul. Here the apostle Paul relates that, when he descended into hell, he saw Judas, who told him that right after he had betrayed Jesus he learned that that was the true Lord, and that was why he had returned the money to the high priests and begged Jesus for forgiveness. Jesus forgave him, sent him into the wilderness and told him to fear no one. But the Devil appeared with gaping jaws before Judas. The latter was frightened and acknowledged the Devil as Lord. After repenting, Judas determined to drown himself, so as to anticipate Jesus in Amenthes (the ancient Egyptian abode of the dead). Jesus reached hell, and brought out every one except Judas. When the keeper of hell, from whom Jesus had wrested the souls of the dead, bewailed the fact to the Devil, the latter told him that there remained to him still one soul. Jesus commanded the archangel Michael to take Judas and put him in Amenthes (Douhet: Dictionnaire des légendes du christianisme, éd. Migne, 120-122. Now a rare edition.).

Notes

1. In Kievska Starina 1889, I: 231-232, there is printed another variant of this Christmas carol in which only the beginning is like the preceding, subsequently the prophet Děva commands a church to be built of "cedar wood".

2. Psellus specifies thus the doctrine of the Euchites, which is close to that of the Zervanites: "The accursed Manes supposed two principles . . . and the Euchites added a third. Their principles are: a father and two sons, the father administers the super-worldly bodies, the younger son the heavenly ones, the older son the worldly ones." (Darmsteter: Ormuzd et Ahriman, 332.) The Euchites or Messalians still survived in Thrace in the X century and eventually were absorbed into the Paulicians. The V century Armenian bishop Eznig sets forth contemporary Armenian legends in which Ahriman invites Ormuzd to dine, and after that the two create the sun (Mikhr, Mithra) to judge the quarrel between their sons (Darmsteter, op. cit. 113).

3. It is imaginable that recollection of the Christmas carol about the apostles' participating in the world-creation may have influenced the introduction of the Ukrainian tale given by Čubinskij (Trudy I: 142-143); but here the narrator, with habitual humor, has introduced such traits as the following: "Once Christ and the Apostle Peter were sitting and they got bored. 'God,' says Peter, 'you always are without something to do, why don't you start to create the world?' 'Fine,' says Christ, 'but we must summon the devil.'" Here we may recall the Christmas carol in which the Lord God and St. Peter are bathing together and start to quarrel as to which is the bigger — the earth or the sky. Peter says it is the earth, God says it is the sky. So God sends three angels to measure the sky and the earth; they find the sky is the larger, as the sky is even while the earth has mountains and valleys (Čubinskij: Trudy III: 307, two variants; Golovackij: Nar. pěsni Galickoj i Ugorskoj Rusi III: 31-32, where the parties are interchanged). Obviously, here God and St. Peter stand in the place of the two Gnostico-apocryphal creators, between whom the upper and the lower kingdoms are divided. The name of the Apostle Peter, it seems to us, is here no accidental occurrence: among the sects similar to the Paulicians the representative to the narrow Judaic trend and the antagonist of the apostle of the heathen, Paul, was hardly popular. It is possible that the often poorly esteemed role which the Apostle Peter plays in the folk tales is an echo of this unpopularity preserved to this day. See Veselovskij: Razyskanija VII: 232, 233 for the Ukrainian and the Roumanian Christmas carols about the quarrel between the apostles.

4. We shall notice that the notion of man's proceeding from God's sweat, but minus any notion of how man's body was formed and minus any dualism, is encountered also in a Serbian tale. Here, in the beginning God was sleeping, then he started to walk about the world until he came to our earth. He perspired, and from his brow there fell a drop which turned into a man (Erben: Sto prostonárodnich pohádek a pověstí slovanských, 257). This tale may be set alongside the Transcaucasian tales of the angels' proceeding from God's tears etc.; but there may also be an influence from the Iranian idea which we have encountered in the tales of the Russian magians.

5. In the Kiev Government there actually is a village Osoti, where there has been found a bronze statuette resembling some which, we know from reliable sources, are often encountered in the mounds of Ossetia and generally throughout the northern slopes of the Caucasus. (The statuette is now in the museum of Kiev University.) Not long ago Sizov" made excavations in these sites (from Novorossijsk" to Suxum") and he has published

the results in the second issue of <u>Materialy po arxeologii Kavkaz</u> under the editorship of Countess Uvarova. We have not had this publication at hand, but in vol. V of <u>Etnografičeskoe Obozrěnie</u> we read the following (p. 199): "The influence of the Persians here (according to Sizov"'s opinion) seems already to have begun in very ancient times and to have expressed itself not only in the appropriation of this and that article but to have penetrated far more deeply. On the basis of the data from burials V. I. Sizov" has succeeded in establishing the fact that in the region extending from the Tsemes valley northward toward Anapa the Zoroastrian religion dominated. If the sheer fact that Mazdaism was confess in the Caucasus is nothing new, since the extent of this cult amor peoples of the Caucasus is known, still what is important about the investigations of V. I. Sizov" is this: (1) the fact that Mazdaism was spread over the region indicated; (2) determination of the date when it held sway; and (3) establishment of the fact that Mazdaism was brought to the region mentioned not from the south but from the north." We should remember that in the Dotar period the ancient Russians were in touch with the Caucasians in Kuban (Tmutrakan) and in Caspia.

6. For the moment let us notice, without recourse to quotations, some of the coincidences between the Ukrainian Christmas carol in which the angels in the form of doves (or a moon) go down to earth to see whether the ancient ceremonies are being maintained (in the later variants, justice and peace between kin and kingdoms) and that place in the Zend-Avesta where the fravashis of the dead (pitri — guardian angels) go to inquire during the feast days between Old and New Year whether praises are still sung to them, whether sacrifices are still offered them, etc (Golovackij: <u>Nar. p. Gal. i Ug. Rusi</u> IV: 60, 112; II: 21; Čubinskij: <u>Trudy</u> III: 414; De Harlez: <u>Avesta</u> 488, Yasht 49-52).

7. We omit making a special citation; the tale should be sought in Veselovskij.

8. Even in the westernmost of the Finno-Turkic variants, the Karelian, there are at any rate ancient details that have been preserved; such as that the devil, when he received from God a small spot on the earth, punched a hole in it; whereupon there crept forth onto the earth all manner of reptiles — a detail that recalls the Bundahish (<u>Etnografičeskoe Obozrěnie</u> XV: 189).

9. We may notice a coincidence for which as yet we have no explanation; namely the similarity between the Altaian tale about the creation of the sun by the devil and the one from Gžat (Smolensk Government) about the creation of sun and moon likewise by the devil (<u>Etnografičeskoe Obozrěnie</u> VII: 263 and X: 239-240). There are no intermediates between the two tales;

yet the power of the devil surpasses in both the power usually attributed to him in the Russian tales and corresponds to what is prevalent in the Altaian tales.

10. See Sbornik za narodno umotvorenie, nauka i knižnina II (1890), III (1890). EWC

6 Evolution of the conceptions about Satan. — The devil. — Earliest biblical conceptions about Satan, the accusing angel; about Azazel, the spirit of the wilderness; about the snake. — Dualism among the Egyptians (Set and his snake) and among the Iranians. — The devil in the later, Greek, books of the Bible; Asmodeus in the Book of Tobit. — Demonology in the apocrypha of Enoch: the war among the angels. — Demonology in the New Testament: Satan, Belial, Belzebul, etc. as Jesus Christ's antagonist. — The serpent (the dragon) of the Apocalypse. — Heosphoros-Lucifer of the prophet Isaiah. — Angelology and demonology of the Talmudists and the Moslems. — Reworking and systematization of the ancient demonological materials by the Christian Church Fathers. — Satan and his angels in the Byzantine-Slavic Palaeae and in other similar books. — The warring of Michael with Satan in the oral Russian tales. — Satanail in the "Discourse of the Three Holy Men" in the Russian and the Bulgarian documents. Innovations in the Bulgarian. — The oral Bulgarian tale about the creation of Paradise by Belzebul. — Parallel Ukrainian tale. — Creation of the angels and the demons according to the "Bundle of Divine Books." — Absence of such a tale among the Balkan Slavs. — Its remote Ukrainian similarities; tales closely similar to it among the Great-Russians and the Finno-Ugric peoples from the Volga to the Altai. — The tale of the spoiling of Adam's body by the devil: the north Russian written tale, the Bulgarian oral tale, the Ukrainian (with the particular episode of the dog), the Great-Russian, the Finno-Ural-Altaian. — Indications of originality in the Altaian tales. — Hypothesis of passage of these tales from the northeast into Russia. — Magyar and Lithuanian variants. — Local elaborations of the Old Bulgarian apocryphas in various Slavic regions. — Variety in the routes and the modes by which the dualistic tales passed from Asia into Europe.

The two Bulgarian oral legends examined above, likewise the legends of the other peoples, and the Liber s. Ioannis, which with some right we may count among the Old Bulgarian monuments, contain curious examples of the general mediaeval and present-day notions of the common folk concerning God and the Devil. In looking over the data of these monuments, in order not to depart from the chief theme (the legends of Satan's diving into the sea after earth) we have had to leave aside the other motifs which are likewise dualistic. Furthermore, the Slavic apocryphas and also the oral literature present other dualistic legends which are akin to those examined thus far. We must turn to them too.

Since it is no longer possible to perceive in these legends remnants from the ancient Slavic mythology, it now becomes clear that we have on our hands a unique mixtum compositum. Which means that we must see into its component elements.

These elements do not fit well into either the frame of churchly-Christian ideas which have grown out of the beginning of European ideas, or into that of the known Greco-Slavic apocryphas. In order to understand correctly the history of how these notions about God and the Devil came about, it is absolutely imperative that we determine their relationship to the Hebrew-Christian. And in order to understand the latter, they must be viewed through a historical method.

The newest literary-critical and historical exegesis shows that among the Hebrews the dualistic ideas about Satan as the Devil and the primeval enemy of God, did not belong to the oldest folk beliefs.[1]

In the Bible, Satan (ha Satan), i.e., the contraposed, the accuser, something like a procurer, appears in the Book of Job among the "Sons of God" (bené ha Elohim; in Greek, angels — oʻι ἄγγελοι τοῦ θεοῦ) who have gathered before Jehovah (I: 6). In the Book of the prophet Zachariah (III: 1-2), Satan stands before Jehovah to accuse the high priest, whom later Jehovah forgives. In Chronicles, one of the last Biblical books, Satan plays the role which in an older book is ascribed to Jehovah himself: in II Samuel XXIV: 1 it is said: "The anger of Jehovah was kindled against Israel, and he moved David against them, saying, Go number"; while in I Chronicles XXI: 1, it is said about the same thing, "Satan stood up against Israel, and moved David to number."[2]

The ancient Hebrews believed in the existence of various spirits (Greek: demons), which lived in the wilderness; but they did not place them in opposition to Jehovah. Even in the Law (Leviticus XVI: 8-10) there is set forth the procedure for an

atonement sacrifice of two buck-goats: the one for Jehovah, the
other for Azazel. The latter (goat) was to be turned loose in
the wilderness for Azazel — obviously the chief spirit of this
wilderness.

The snake in the familiar place about the sin of Eve and
Adam in the Book of Genesis (III: 1-15) has nothing in common
with Satan or with Azazel and spirits like him. It is simply one
of the earthly animals — "the serpent, more subtle than any
beast of the field," which Jehovah curses "above all cattle and
above every beast of the field." But this story cannot be counted
as belonging to the most ancient Hebrew folk-traditions, for its
aspect is in conflict with the worship of the serpent-image among
the Hebrews. Even when the Biblical books were being edited,
the Hebrews ascribed to Moses himself the making of the serpent of brass, which the Hebrews were to look upon, when
they were bitten by fiery serpents, when "Jehovah sent fiery
serpents among the people" (Numbers XXI: 6-9). In II Kings
XVIII: 4 it is said that this image was kept in the temple at
Jerusalem down to the time of King Hezekiah, who broke it because "unto those days the children of Israel did burn incense
to it." The Biblical tales, obviously, soften the fact that among
the most ancient Hebrews there was a formal cult of God in the
form of a snake. The basis of the name of the angels called
seraphim is the word seraph, i.e., snake. It is notable that
even Josephus Flavius, at the end of the I century A.D., still
holds to the ancient notions. In transmitting, with slight change,
the tale in the Book of Genesis about the expulsion of Adam and
Eve from paradise, he sees in their tempter only the snake, and
ascribes to it only envy at human happiness (Antiquit. Judaicae
I: 1).

Meanwhile, among the ancient eastern peoples dualism went
on developing systematically, the rudiments of which exist in
all the mythologies. Along with this, the dark and evil God, or
(after the rudiments of philosophical theology had progressed),
the earthly, material god, set over against the heavenly, ideal,
began by many peoples to be represented as a snake. Thus Set-
Typhon was represented among the Egyptians, the adversary of
Osiris, conquered at last by Osiris' son Horus; after which Osiris resurrects and becomes king and judge over the dead. This
Set, among other things, was represented also in the form of
the snake Apopis.[3]

Of the Iranian dualism and the meaning in it of the snake, which is the chief progeny if not the image of Ahriman, we have had much occasion to speak in this study. In Iran the dualism with a definite role for the snake developed most systematically.[4]

Such Iranian dualistic ideas are noticed among the Hebrews at a very late epoch, not only right after the Babylonian captivity and the Persian sovereignty, but also in the Alexandrine epoch. The first Hebrew monument in which we see traces of dualistic ideas is the so-called Book of the Wisdom of Solomon, which in its oldest edition exists only in the Greek language, and goes back to the I century B. C. Here it is said that God first created man indestructible, but "through envy of the devil (διαβόλου) came death into the world; and they that do hold of his side do find it." (Wisdom II: 23-24). Here the reference probably is to murder. The word διάβολος is the rendition of the name Satan in the Greek translation of the Bible, which was probably done in the II century B.C. The Greek word διάβολος, slanderer, confirms the first meaning of the word Satan — adversary.

In the Book of Tobit, which exists in ancient edition likewise only in the Greek language, and is counted among the apocryphas by the strict Biblicists, there is featured a special demoniac personage Asmodeus, whose power shatters the angel Raphael.[5]

Marked progress in the development of demonology and in the reworking of the ancient Hebrew traditions in a dualistic spirit is represented by the Book of Enoch. This book is preserved in Ethiopian (Abyssinian); translated, apparently, from Greek. In this book, which is extremely important also for the explanation of other apocryphas, among them also the Slavic, there is a reworking, among other things, in a dualistic context the short tale (inserted in the Bible before the Deluge) of how the "giants" were produced: "the sons of God (bené ha Elohim; in the Greek translation it became υἱοὶ τοῦ θεοῦ) saw the daughters of men that they were fair, and they took them wives of all that they chose. . . . The giants (in Greek translation, οἱ γίγαντες) were on the earth at that time; they proceeded from that the sons of God went in unto the daughters of men, and the latter bore them children." (Genesis VI: 2, 4).[6]

The Book of Enoch tells this legend similarly: When the children of men multiplied, there were born to them shapely and fair daughters. And when the angels saw the heavenly children, they were enamored of them, and they said one to another:

Come let us choose wives of the race of man and let us beget
children of them. Then Samias their chief (a name unknown to
the Bible) said: I fear me that you shall not be able to accomplish
that which you have thought, and that upon me alone shall fall
the punishment of your transgression. But they said to him: We
put ourselves under oath to thee. And truly they took oath to him
and bound themselves with binding oaths. They were in number
200 and they let themselves down upon Arodes, a place which is
nigh unto the mountain Armon. — The Book of Enoch gives further on the names of the principal of these angels and relates
what they taught people: how to make weapons, ornaments, fine
arts, arched bows (this Azazel taught), magic, astronomy, etc.
Then Michael, Gabriel,[7] Raphael et al. when they heard the cla-
mor of the people who were suffering from iniquity, turned with
laments to the Most High. The Most High sends one of the angels
to Noah, to inform him of the Deluge, and he says to Raphael:
Take Azazel, tie his hands and feet, and hurl him into darkness
and leave him in the wilderness Dudael; let fall upon him heavy
and sharp rocks, cover him with darkness. Let him stay there
forever and let him not see the light, and when the Day of Judgment shall come, plunge him into the fire." . . . Then God said
to Michael: "Go proclaim the punishment that shall overtake
Samias and all those who had a part in this transgression, who
have had union with women. . . . When their children shall have
been done away [the giants], . . . fasten them down for the dura-
tion of 70 generations, until the Day of Judgment and the End of
all things, and the sequel of this judgment shall be eternal for
them: they shall then be hurled into the depth of the fire, which
shall torment them without let, and there they shall remain forever." (Enoch VII-XI, Dictionnaire des apocryphes, Migne I:
427-434). The Book of Enoch, or at any rate its stories, were
known to the author of the Epistle of Jude; for in it is said that
"angels that kept not their own principality, but left their proper
habitation (God) hath kept in everlasting bonds under darkness
unto the judgment of the great day" (v. 6). We read this kind of
thing in the II Epistle of Peter (II: 4), where the place into which
are cast down those who sinned, who are surrounded by darkness
as though bound in chains, is called Tartarus.[8]

In the New Testament books, which have come down to us,
as we know, in the Greek language, and which in all probability
were originally written in that language, we find much

demonological material. In the Epistles of the apostle Paul, there is mentioned, among other things, the "prince of powers of the air"; which prince is active in rebellious people ('ἄρχων τῆς ἐχουσίας τοῦ 'αέρος τούτου; Ephesians II: 2), and of the angel of Satan ('ἄγγελος Σατανᾶ) who buffets the apostle (II Corinthians XII: 7); and of Beliel (Syrian: malice), as the antithesis of Christ, just as darkness is the antithesis of light, and unrighteousness of righteousness. (See II Corinthians VI: 14-15.)

In the synoptic gospels, beside the various unnamed evil spirits, there is special mention of Beelzebub, prince of the demons (Βελζεβούλ 'ἄρχων τῶν δαμιονίων — Matthew XII: 24; cf. IX: 34; Mark III: 22; Luke XI: 15, 18, 19). This Beelzebub (in the Bulgarian tale, Zerzebulo) is made up out of the Old Testament Beelzebub, or more correctly Baal Zebub, god of the Philistine city Ekron, to whom the king Ahaziah sent to inquire concerning his illness (II Kings I: 2, 3, 16). Beside this, there is often met the Devil who is referred to especially in the prophesy of the Last Judgment, in the spirit of the Book of Enoch: "When the Son of man shall come in his glory, and all the angels with him," to judge "all the nations," he shall say to the sinners: "Depart from me, ye cursed, into the eternal fire which is prepared for the devil and his angels" (Matt. XXV: 31, 41). In the Gospel of St. Luke Christ says to Peter, after the Last Supper (XXII: 31-32): "Simon, Simon, behold, Satan asked to have you, that he might sift you as wheat; but I made supplication for thee," etc. The devil is brought upon the scene as the tempter of Jesus in the important tale of the sojourn of the latter in the wilderness, where the angels are placed over against this Devil (Matt. IV: 1-11. Likewise Luke IV: 2-13). In the corresponding place in Mark (I: 13), the Devil is called Satan.[9]

In the Gospel of Luke (X: 18), we find words of Jesus that during the Middle Ages became the point of departure for entire demonological depictions: "I beheld Satan fallen as lightning from heaven."

In the Revelation of John (XII), we find a tale which also became that kind of rich source for mediaeval demonological ideas. "And a great sign was seen in heaven: a woman arrayed with the sun, and the moon under her feet, and upon her head a crown of twelve stars; and she was with child; and she cried out, travailing in birth, and in pain to be delivered. And there was seen another sign in heaven: and behold, a great red dragon, having

seven heads and ten horns, and upon his heads seven diadems.
And his tail draweth the third part of the stars of heaven, and
did cast them to the earth: and the dragon standeth before the
woman that is about to be delivered, that when she is delivered
he may devour her child. And she was delivered of a son, a
man child, who is to rule all the nations with a rod of iron: and
her child was caught up unto God, and unto his throne. And the
woman fled into the wilderness, where she hath a place prepared
of God, that there they may nourish her a thousand two hundred
and threescore days. And there was war in heaven: Michael and
his angels going forth to war with the dragon; and the dragon
warred and his angels; and they prevailed not, neither was their
place found any more in heaven. And the great dragon was cast
down, the old serpent, he that is called the Devil and Satan ('ο
δράκων 'ο μέγας, 'ο 'όφις 'ο 'αρχαῖος, 'ο καλούμενος διάβολος καὶ
Σατανᾶς), the deceiver of the whole world; he was cast down to
the earth, and his angels were cast down with him. And I heard
a great voice in heaven, saying, Now is come the salvation, and
the power, and the kingdom of our God, and the authority of his
Christ; for the accuser of our brethren is cast down, who ac-
cuseth them before our God. . . . Therefore rejoice, O heavens,
and ye that dwell in them. Woe for the earth and for the sea:
because the devil is gone down unto you, having great wrath,
knowing that he hath but a short time."

After this is described the grievous attack of the dragon upon
the woman, whom the earth defended, new visions of the apostle
(a beast resembling in its parts a leopard, a bear, a lion, etc.)
and then — the subduing of the dragon: "And I saw an angel coming down out of heaven, having the key of the abyss and a great
chain in his hand. And he laid hold on the dragon, the old serpent, which is the Devil and Satan, and bound him for a thousand
years, and cast him into the abyss, and shut it, and sealed it
over him, that he sould deceive the nations no more, until the
thousand years should be finished: after this he must be loosed
for a little time. (Rev. XX: 1-3).

In the same circle of Johannine monuments we find the notion of the evil spirit as the Prince of the World, the antagonist
of Jesus the Word. After Lazarus' resurrection, there is heard,
before a multitude of people, the voice of God from heaven: "I
have both glorified it, and will glorify it again!" Then Jesus said,
"Now is the judgment of this world; now shall the prince of this

world ('ο ἄρχων τοῦ κόσμου τούτου) be cast out." (John XII: 28, 31-32.) When they are about to arrest Jesus, he says: "the prince of the world cometh" (John XIV: 30). Promising to send to his disciples from his father a new comforter ('ο παράκλητος), Jesus says that the prince of this world has been judged (John XVI: 11). From these words they drew the notion that the devil had a special part in the crucifixion of Christ and that Christ and his ambassador were victorious over him.

These are the materials out of which is composed the Christian systematic demonology. About these the commentators on the materials have gathered still other materials of various derivation. Among the latter a special place in the Christian eschatology is held by the interpretation that is given to the comparison of the Babylonian king with the morning-star ('εωσφορος, φώσφορος, lucifer), which occurs at the end of the Book of Isaiah. The Hebrew writer is exulting because the Medes (the Persians) have overthrown the greatness of Babylon, and among other things he says: "How art thou fallen, O day-star, son of the morning! How art thou cut down to the ground, that didst lay low the nations! And thou saidst in thy heart, I will ascend into heaven, I will exalt my throne above the stars of God; and I will sit upon the mount of congregation, in the uttermost parts of the north; I will ascend above the heights of the clouds; I will make myself like the Most High. Yet thou shalt be brought down to Sheol, to the uttermost parts of the pit. They that see thee shall gaze at thee, they shall consider thee, saying, Is this the man that made the earth to tremble, that did shake kingdoms; that made the world as a wilderness, and overthrew the cities thereof; that let not loose his prisoners to their home?" (Isaiah XIV: 12-17).[10] In this fragment there are hints of the Babylonian or Chaldeo-Iranian cosmogonic notions, which at some time, in some way or another, could have been shared also by the Hebrews.

Ordinarily the stars and the planets, as luminous objects, are reckoned among the good divinities, but sometimes the mythic symbolism, even the naive symbolism, and by so much more the astrological one, looks upon the stars as allies of the night, enemies of the light, that is, of the God of the sun, the day, the heaven. Such an idea penetrated also into the Vedas, where Usanas (the morning-star) is called the antagonist of the sun, and Indra the abductor of the heavenly cows, etc.[11]

In Chaldea, especially in later times, apace with the development of a systematic astrology, the planets, being lights with irregular courses as compared with the fixed stars, began to be counted as beings that were harmful to the gods of the upper region and of the people. In one of the later Iranian books, Minokered, the seven planets are held forth as the weapons of Ahriman, who with their aid transfers to the evil ones the treasure assigned by fortune to the good.[12]

It is very possible that when the book of the prophet Isaiah was written, there were in the Chaldeo-Hebrew circles similar ideas about the harmfulness of the most brilliant planet for the heavenly god around the northern mountain; around which, according to many eastern cosmogonies, the stars revolve; although in this matter the passage given above from the book of Isaiah is not quite clear. At all events, the major part of the imagery in this passage refers to the Babylonian king, while the planet itself is mentioned only for the sake of comparison. But, when the Judeo-Christian demonology was being laid down, this passage was interpreted as the account of the pride and fall of the Daystar or Lucifer, which had already become a personage and identified with that Satan whose fall Jesus saw, according to the Gospel of Luke. Afterward this story appropriated the imagery from the Book of Enoch and from the Revelation of John, about the conflict between the angels and the demons, and was carried back to the beginning of the world, to the time between the creation and fall of Adam. At the same time John's already completed identification of the ancient serpent with the dragon which the angels kill, had gotten under way.

It is very possible that when all these Old and New Testament elements were being interpreted and fused into an integrated system, there were present in the Judeo-Christian circles complete dualistic tales as well, which were only awaiting confirmation from the authors of the sacred writings. To impartial thinking it is clear that syncretistic elements from various eastern dualistic beliefs must have taken part in them.

Thus was formed an entire demonological epos, of which the sundry variants are perceived in the mediaeval Christian writers and artists, among the Hebraic Talmudists and the Moslems, and which influenced also the ancient written narratives and oral tales that are found now also among the Slavs, especially the Balkan and Russian Slavs.

The Talmudic tales place the conflict between Jehovah and his angel Satan, who rebelled against him, at the beginning of creation. In this way the composers of the Talmud seek to fill out the Biblical tale of the world-creation; for the Bible says nothing about the origin of the angels, whom it presents directly, as already-existent entities, under the name of "children of God," "man of God" (meleak Elohim; sometimes simply a form of the god himself — Elohim) or "gods" (elohim). (For instances see Piepenbring, op.cit.; also Maurice Vernès: Du prétendu polithéisme hébreu, passim.) Contrariwise, the Iranian books tell how each of the gods, Ormuzd and Ahriman, creates his own angels. At the same time, these gods themselves are taken to be coeternal from the beginning; later (among the Zervanites), as born of one deity.

According to the Talmudists, the angels as well as the demons are created earlier than men; according to some, on the first day of creation along with the firmament and fire; according to others, on the fifth, along with the birds. Some Talmudic rabbis assume that the demons were created on the sixth day of creation, on Sabbath eve, and that that is why they turned out worthless and evil as compared with the angels.[13] According to the teaching of the majority of the rabbis, the angels, besides, are created by God for daily service, while the demons were also the fruit of unions of Adam and Eve with the demons, and so they continue to reproduce.[14]

From among the Talmudic opinions concerning the angels and the demons, some deserve special mention because they resemble the popular Christian and Moslem notions, which in all probability have been infused under the direct or indirect influence of these Talmudic opinions.

Thus, among the Talmudists we find an original development of one passage in the Book of the prophet Daniel. The symbolic succession of the four kingdoms which held sway in Hither Asia are represented in the Hebrew book as four beasts; and it pictures God the dispenser of judgments as an old man sitting on a fiery throne, while a fiery river pours forth from before him; a thousand thousands serve him and ten thousand millions stand before him (Dan. VII: 9-10). On this passage the Talmudists rest the notion that beside the first-created angels, thousands emanate every day from the fiery stream for the service of God.[15] Analogous with these notions are those which farther on we shall find among the Turkic and Slavic peoples: God creates angels by hammering them out, or by striking fiery sparks from a stone. These analogies are explainable on the assumption that the Hebrew notions as well as the Turkic could have had a common source; for instance, in the Iranian East.

According to some Talmudic rabbis, the demons that were created on the sixth day, Sabbath eve, were formed of drops of Adam's semen[16] — a notion analogous to those which, farther on, we shall see in the Slavic oral tales. According to the latter, the Devil creates Adam from the drops which fall from his fingers.

In the Talmudic books there are tales of how some of the angels or demons did not want God to create man. God burned up the discontented angels or turned them into demons, and then he showed them that man is more intelligent than they, because he called all animals by name while the angels had been unable to do this.[17]

These stories passed in a somewhat altered form into the Koran and other Moslem books: in the Koran, God, after telling the angels that Adam was more intelligent than they, commanded them all to bow down before him; all agreed except Iblis, who said: "You created me out of fire, and him out of clay."[18] Hence the enmity of Satan-Iblis toward Adam, hence the seduction of Adam and the fall of Satan-Iblis.

In the Talmudists' demonology the legendary subjects increase markedly, and many of them must have been taken over from the peoples neighboring the Hebrews; but the bases of this demonology have remained true to the ancient Hebraic traditions. To the point, — in this demonology there is but little that is properly dualistic: the demons appear most often as purposely created by God. Some rabbis even assume circumcised demons who believe and who know the law. According to others, the demons will serve the Messiah as punishers of the unrighteous peoples; or again, after a time they shall be cleansed and turned into angels.[19]

We see many more dualistic ideas in the ancient Christian literature which was expanding the notions of the Helleno-Hebraic literature, and obviously was more exposed to the influence of various more or less Hellenized strata of the population in the various parts of Hither Asia and North Africa. The dualistic notions of the Christian-Gnostics are well known.

The Gnostics interpreted in a dualistic sense even the first words of the Biblical tale of the world-creation, saying that the Darkness in this tale means the Devil, and the Light the Son of God who emanated from God and who appeared after Satan, just as among the Zervanites Ormuzd is born after Ahriman.[20] The Church Fathers, who defended the more strictly monotheistic teaching, fought against such interpretations and against the more out-and-out dualism in general; but they gave recognition to its weaker forms; therefore they set Satan rather high, and filled out the Biblical tale of the creation of the angels, among whom they placed Satan in an important position. According to the teaching of Lactantius, Irenius, et al., God first created a spirit like himself, and later another, in whom the divine holiness did not sustain itself: this was Satan, who also turned man away from good to evil.[21]

As early as the III-IV centuries the Church Fathers composed an integrated dogmatic doctrine out of the materials of the Old and New Testament demonologies, which we have presented above. The angels are created before man, the demons are derived from fallen angels. Their sin consists in that they let themselves be led by Heosphorus-Lucifer, who became prideful and sought to make himself equal with God. Into this drama, which proceeds before the creation of man, is inserted the battle of the archangel Michael and the other angels who are faithful to God; a battle which in the Book of Enoch is placed in the epoch before the flood; and the fight of Michael with the dragon, which the Apocalyptist places in the future. The Devil-Satan's temptation of Eve is the consequence of this sin of Satan-Lucifer and his being thrown out of heaven.[22]

The Byzantian writers summarized these notions of the Church Fathers in the treatises whose object was to transmit in compact form the Biblical story of the world-creation, filled out with new materials. Such treatises, called Paleae, passed over to the Slavs. In a copy of a Slavo-Russian Palea in a XVI century manuscript, Porfirjev finds the following characteristic tale about Satan, which he transcribes in his Apokrifičeskija skazanija o vetxozavětnyx" litsax" i sobytijax" po rukopisam" Soloveckoj biblioteki, 83-85.

In the tale of the creation of the fourth day, it says:

Now on this day, one of the archangels, named
Satanaïl, who was the leader of the 10th cohort, saw
that God had beautified this firmament by his word,
and the earth. And he exalted himself with pride and
said within his thought: How beautiful is this sub-
heaven! And I see no living thing upon it; let me go
down to earth and let me take over its rule and I shall
be as (a) god. And I will set my throne on the clouds.
Straightway did the Lord cast him down from heaven
for the pride of his thought; and with him fell those
that were under him, the tenth cohort. Like sand they
did rain down from heaven. And they pierced through
to the infernal depth; some of them moreover were on
the earth; some the archangelic voice suspended in the
air. This <u>Archistrategos</u> Michael was the chief and
captain of the Lord's forces, the commander of the
second cohort. As he saw the backslider falling with
his cohort, he spoke forth with a sonorous voice strongly and terribly: We acknowledge and with a voice of
might we praise the God of all. He spoke: We acknowledge that we are created for service by him. And
standing before God (we acknowledge) that in which you
raged and what you perpetrated. He spoke: We acknowledge (this), serving God with trembling. He
spoke: We acknowledge that the light is with us. And
now are ye separated from the light and are become
darkness. He spoke: We acknowledge that God the
Light is with us the divine servants of his terrible
might. Then the demons having heard the voice of the
archangel forthwith were suspended in the aether. And
the first of these fallen demons pierced through to the
infernal regions and they are as deaf, and these from
down there are aware of nothing in the world. And of
those who among them fell upon the earth, these as
they go about on the earth work evil with their spells.
The last of them the archangelic voice placed in the
aether. And these also who now are suspended do work
whatever evils they are capable of working. And of
these all Satan was the chief of the cohort, he also was
among them. He was the overseer of the earthly cohort and had received from God the charge of caring
for the earth. And this Satan who fell sinned in his
thought. And he styled himself the adversary of God,
so in his place the Lord put the chief Michael. The
fallen cohort was termed demons. And from them the
Lord took their glory and honor and brightness which

had been theirs before and he placed them in a dark
spirit(?), and commanded them to fly about in the air.
And in the place of the fallen tenth cohort God bethought
to create man. And the brilliance and the crown of the
fallen the Lord God gave over to the right believers,
and they of the tenth cohort are called the well-disposed-
toward-man.

The tale that Porfirjev adduces after this one is taken from
a later manuscript (XVIII century) containing various articles;
but in its imagery perhaps it is older; for in places it recalls the
Bundahish. It remains to be settled whether the imagery in this
tale has proceeded from written monuments, and if so, out of
what kin; or, if not, out of what oral tales, and if so where: in
the Balkan peninsula or in Russia?

"On the fifth day God created the sun and the moon
and ten stars and in this same day Satan fell from grace
and Satanail saw heaven and earth y-dight and thought
within himself: I will create for myself a throne in the
clouds and I shall be like unto the Most High, that my
rout may give me glory. And he created for himself
a throne on the northern clouds[23] and exalted himself
and he was then voyevod of an angelic rout. And God
saw his adversary and God sent Michael the archangel
and bade him cast down Satanail. And Michael came
unto Satanail and saw in him a great divinity and he did
not dare to look upon him. And Michael went to God
and said, Great Lord, thy divinity is upon him. And
the Lord took away from him the divinity and said, Go
cast him down. And Michael went and saw Satanail
like as a common man and he struck him with a scepter
and overthrew his throne and hurled Satan down and
with all of his forces and the Lord took from him the
divinity and took silt away from him. And the Lord gave
the silt to the angels and to the Archangel, and he called
the name of Micha Michael.[24] And he gave to him the
seniority over all the heavenly powers and he called the
name of the transgressor Satan Devil. And Satan was
darkened with his forces and he went above. And he
lashed the earth and sought to pasture in heaven and
Michael said: Lord, the heavens are going to move.
And the Lord said unto him, Forbid it with a word. And
Michael said, Lord, What dost thou wish me to say?
And the Lord said, Utter forth a Holy of Holies (one
Lord Jesus Christ in the glory of God the Father. Amen);
he quickly spoke out thus. And then all the heavenly

powers sang forth: One holy, one Lord Jesus Christ in the glory of God the Father. Amen. And then were the heavens confirmed. And Satan then came to the earth and heard the voice of Michael and was in hell in the abyss under the earth, and under it the water, and under the water fire unquenchable. And those who were close to him, they with him pierced through the earth to the infernal hell and nevermore can they come forth, and they can do nothing and they walk in darkness and to eternity they do not see the earth. Others yet fell on the earth and they heard the voice of Michael and they remained on the earth and they walk about below the heavens and they ever do evil to the generations of man and they change themselves into madmen. Others yet did not come to the earth and hearing the voice of Michael they remained in the air. And their chief is a devil savage of heart, a man of war and constantly they hold (in their) self-exaltation an exceedingly insatiable desire for evil, they incite to evil without any cause" (there follows the matter of the madmen, with a citation to the vision of St. Cyprian, and about the angelic ranks).

We find similar imagery about the battle between Michael and Satan in the narrative of the Tiberian sea (Porfirjev, op.cit., 88-89) and in the Bundle of Divine Books (Pypin: Istorija slavjanskix" literatur" I: 81), apparently in a later and compilatory rendition; at all events not quite full but compact. In the Svitok of Pypin it is interesting that Michael receives power to conquer Satanail only when God shears him to be a monk and bestows a schema — traits which, in our opinion, are very late and not Bogomil.

Very close to the second tale of the Solovec manuscripts is the White-Russian oral tale in Romanov: Belorusskij Sbornik" IV: 1-2. The influence of such manuscripts upon the Great-Russian tales mentioned above (ch. V), and transcribed by Barsov and Derunov (see Veselovskij: Razyskanija IX-XVII: 70-72) is clearly visible; so also in the Ukrainian tales from the Kharkov government, printed in books XIII-XIV of Etnografičeskoe Obozrěnie: 76-78. In the latter, it appears to us, we must see an example of the growing influence of the Great-Russian Raskolniks upon the Ukrainians.

Of the other Old Slavic renditions of this story, the brief renditions in the various copies of the Beseda trex" svjatitelej are noteworthy. The Old Russian indices of the prohibited book make out the Bulgarian priest and celebrated Bogomil, Eremias, to have been the composer of these discourses (see Močul'skij in Russk. Fil. Vestnik I (1887): 133; Porfirjev: Apokrifičeskija skazanija o novozavětnyx'' licax'' i sobytijax'', 120-121). In one copy of the "Beseda," printed by Močul'skij, from a manuscript which Grigorovič received from Čeboksarov'', and in which there was a variant taken from the "Bundle of Divine Books", the derivation of Satan is represented in a very dualistic spirit:

Qu. Out of what was Satan born?

Ans. On the Tiberian sea in the ninth wave was he born.

Qu. When was Satan cast down?

Ans. Before the creation of Adam, for four days then because of his pride he fell from the glory of God and was called Satan devil. (Russk. Fil. Věstn. IV (1887): 178).

We cannot leave this extract without noting that the citation to the Tiberian sea does not seem to us to be original in the Beseda. First, — the Tiberian sea could have risen to the level of a primeval ocean sooner in Russia than in Bulgaria; the latter being more bookish and nearer to Palestine in the Middle Ages. Next, in the other copies of the Beseda the passage concerning the former primacy of Satan is edited more compactly. Thus, in the copy printed by Porfirjev in his Apokrifičeskija skazanija o novozavětnyx'' licax'' i sobytijax'' po rukopisjam'' Soloveckoj biblioteki, this passage reads thus: "Grigorij said: Whom did God name first on the earth? Vasilij said: Satan was the first angel and for his pride he was cast down from heaven before the creation of Adam and is called Satan and devil." In the copy printed by Pypin (Ložnyja i otrečennyja knigi russkoj stariny 169-171) this passage reads even more exactly: Grigorij said: Who first was given a name on earth? Vasilij said: Satanail was first named and he was reckoned. . . among the angels, but for his pride he was named Satan-devil, the angel cast forth from heaven onto the earth before the creation of Adam for four days."

In the Bulgarian copy of the "Discourse of the Three Prelates": "Questions and the answer of the great Vasilij, Grigorij the theologian and John Chrysostomus about. . ."[25] printed by the celebrated Serbian scholar St. Novaković, along with other articles in the Bulgarian anthology of the XVIII century, which is in Belgrade, we find the following interesting tale about the devil:

"How did God create the devil?

Answer. When he created the heaven and the earth, and God saw his shadow and he said: Come forth, brother, to be with me. He came forth like a man, and his name was called Samuel.

Question. How did he fall away from God?

Answer. When God was building paradise, and Samuel was stealing from whatever he commanded that they build, from all the fruits a seed, and carried them away that he might build in secret from God. And the Lord said: Thou stealest from me; let it be for thy banishment. Samuel came forth and said: Lord, bless what we have built. Whatever is blessed, there am I in the midst of it. And Samail went to see also that tree which he had stolen and planted, and when he saw it, then Samail's cutting of that tree had wilted away. (Starine, VI: 489. Bugarski zbornik, pisan prošloga vieka narodnim jezikom).[26]

Although this copy of the Discourse is written late and in the popular tongue, obviously it is constructed after an older Church-Slavic copy. And what is interesting is the fact that there is in it no mention of the Tiberian sea, as is also the case in most of the Russian copies of the Discourse. This strengthens our doubt that the Russian story of the Tiberian sea, of the diving Satanail, etc. is of ancient Bulgarian origin. Instead, the Bulgarian copy of the Discourse gives an interesting detail about the conflict of the devil with God, which we do not find in the other Slavic copies.

We think that this detail does not belong at all to the remnants of the ancient Bogomil literature, but has been inserted by the author of the Bulgarian copy of the Discourse from the oral tales. Yet these tales must have come to Bulgaria independently of the Bogomil literature. In the latter the devil is called Satanail. But he is called Samail in the later Asiatic tales, e.g., in the above-cited Trans-Caucasian, and in the traces of Talmudic stories, where Samael is the name of the angel of death (see the Rabbinic stories of the life of Moses, printed in Gfroerer: Prophaetae veteres pseudoepigraphi; cf. Porfirjev: Apokrifičeski skazanija o vetxozavětn. lits. i sobyt., 61-67).

In the other monuments of the apocryphal literature, only one parallel to the Bulgarian book-tale of how Samuel planted his trees can be pointed out; it is the tale in the Vision of Baruch concerning the time when God commanded the angels to plant trees in paradise, whereupon Satanail planted a vineyard there, from which Adam tasted (Opisanie slavjanskix" rukopisej Moskovskoj Sinodal'noj biblioteki, otd. II, 3, #330, pp. 752-

754). But this is a different story, albeit composed in the same
spirit.

Again in the Bulgarian oral literature, we find a tale with
the same theme as in the Beseda; except that it is more expanded. This is the excellent tale from Prilep, communicated by
M. Cepenkov in Sbornik za narodni umotvorenija etc. I: iii
97-98.

"The Lord drove the Zerzevulo with his angels out
of paradise and cursed them, that they be black and dark,
and that their seat be in eternal torment. Zerzevulo
from eternal torment looked at paradise and it was very
painful to him. And for his angels it was painful and
many times they asked him: Ah, what have you done,
Zerzevul, why did you sin against the Lord that he drove
us from paradise, and put us in eternal torment!" And
it was very painful to Zerzevul, that his angels asked
him thus.

He thought, and he thought, what should he do, and
he figured it out, so he made the devils to make a heaven too. They made it, they built it, in every way like
the paradise of the Lord. They took from all the trees
and flowers that were in the paradise of the Lord and
they set them out. When it was done, Zerzevul looked
it over from all the gates and he liked it very much.
"Ho my band, have you seen that we too can make a
paradise like what God can make? Come, go in, eat,
drink, of everything that is inside; I don't forbid you
anything, the way the Lord forbade something to the
man he put inside to live with his wife; I give you free-
dom to do whatever you want to do. Say this to the people: whatever any one wants to do let him command.
In my paradise there is food, drink, pleasure-seeking,
as much as they ask of me.

Some days went by, and they heard some voices of
the angels who were in paradise, as they sang before
the Lord. "Ah, say, Master Zerzevul," said the angels
to him, "we have great pain when we hear the angels
singing over there before the Lord. Why did you make
paradise so close to the paradise of the Lord? Find out
some means that we do not hear from over there beautiful songs that they are singing. Alas, find out a means
to do this."

When Zerzevul heard the plaints of the devils, a
great woe fell upon him and immediately he gathered
all about him. "Listen to us," he said to them, "you
are my angels: If you are my faithful servants, I want

you to obey me in what I tell you. You take your orders from me, Zerzevul, and I command you by my name and by the crown with the two horns that is on my head, that you now make a tower high up to heaven, so that we may climb up and kill the Lord, so that the angels will have no one to sing to." "We are obedient to your name and we give homage before you to your horns." "Honor brings honor," said Zerzevul to them; "Let horns appear on you too, let them be wreathes to your heads." And immediately there grew horns on them.

In three days they built the tower and on the following morning Zerzevul was to kill the Lord. The morning came and at the command of God the tower bent backward, and Zerzevul could not enter it. He gave orders to straighten it. They straightened it three times, and it always acted that way. On the fourth time the Lord let it stay, and he climbed up with all the devils and started to shoot an arrow at God. As soon as he shot it, it turned back and struck him on the head and cut it off. He screamed, he yelled. Dismay fell upon all of them, they all began to hop about on one foot, and from then on they began to be called by people "one-feet."

As soon as they saw that they could do nothing to the Lord, they began to climb down from the tower. The Lord commanded, and the tower with all of them fell down into the depth of the earth and into an eternal torment, like a huge cauldron full of tar and filth, to cook Zerzevul and all of his. They cooked in it, and from then to this day they have been cooking. But the paradise that they had planted with all kinds of trees and flowers, all were turned into thorns and hawthorns and barren stones. And there opened up an abyss between the paradise of the Lord and the thorny paradise of Zerzevul (or the eternal devil's-abode), so that they should not be able to fly so that they could not approach from the one side or the other."

The first half of this tale is composed in the spirit of the Book of St. John. Probably the formation of the second half has been influenced by echoes of the Biblical story of the Tower of Babel.

In the Ukraine (the Podol government) there is recorded an (incomplete) tale which has preserved the recollection of only the second half of this Bulgarian legend.

"Once the oldest devil thought to make himself equal with God. So he commanded the devils to raise up a big tower. When

the tower was finished, all the devils climbed up, so as to rejoice at their work; but God destroyed their building for them,
and the devils flew from that place forty days and forty nights,
and wherever each one fell there he is till now, and he has gotten his name from the place where he fell: the water-, the moun-
tain-, the muddy-, the plains-, the canebrake- (devil), etc."
(Čubinskij, Trudy eksped. I: 191).

For the present, it cannot be determined where this legend
was definitely put together: whether in Bulgaria, or somewhere
farther east.

In the "Bundle of Divine Books" as edited by Pypin, — after
the tale of Satanail's diving into the sea for sand and flint so that
God might create the land, there comes a tale of the creation of
the angels and the devils.

"And the Lord having taken flint, he brake it in twain; in
his right hand the Lord kept that for himself, and out of the left
hand did he give unto Satanail. And the Lord took sand [sic],
and began to strike out of this flint, and the Lord said: Fly out,
angels and archangels and all ye that are the hosts of heaven in
shape and likeness; and there began to fly from this flint sparks
of fire and the Lord created angels and archangels and all the
nine ranks.

And Satanail saw what the Lord had created, and he began
to strike the flint which God had given from his left hand, and
there began to fly forth for Satanail his angels and Satanail
created a power in the Heavens. Then did the Lord make Satanail the chief over all his angelic ranks; Satan's power he placed
in the tenth rank." According to the copy of Buslaev, when the
Lord struck the flint with his mace "there flew forth clean spirits," while from the other half of the flint Satan "hewed a numberless raging rout of carnal gods" (Pypin: Istorija slavjanskix"
literatur" I: 80).

A similar thing is told more briefly in the Bundle of Divine
Books, printed by Močul'skij (Russk. Fil. Věstn. IV (1887):
174).

We know of no such tale existing among the Balkan peoples.

Among the Ukrainians there is something only remotely
similar: St. Peter, grateful to the devil for having carried him
about the earth cross-wise, teaches the devil how to make help-
ers for himself: "Rise early on Saturday, take water and sprinkle it behind you; as much as you sprinkle, so many devils will

come into being." (Čubinskij: Trudy ekspeditsii I: 143). Or:
God told the devil to wet his finger in water and throw a drop of
water behind him, without looking around. The devil did this,
but he could not refrain from looking around, and he saw a devil
like himself. He started to carry the experiment further, and
there sprang up numberless devils (op. cit., 190-191). In a tale
recorded in the Podol government, i.e., in a place not far from
the Balkan Slavs, the creation of the devils by such means is assigned to Adam: The Lord, without considering carefully, stuck
between Adam's legs a piece of the clay which had been left over
from the creation, and so there came into being the "sinful body."
Adam began to beg God for a woman. The Lord did not want to
give him a woman, but wanted to give him a friend instead, and
said to him: Wet your little finger with dew and flip it before you,
and you shall obtain a friend; but be careful not to toss it behind
you! Adam forgot, wet his whole hand and tossed it behind him
— and up jumped five devils. As soon as Adam saw them, he
started to run away, and the devils began to wet their nails and
to toss them behind. Thereupon they multiplied so much that
even the heaven began to pop." (Dragomanov: Malorusskija
narodnyja predanija, etc.: 91).

In contrast to the Ukraine, in Great-Russia there are tales
of the creation similar to those we find in the Bundle of Divine
Books. They have been transcribed in the research of Veselovskij. Such is the tale from the Olenets government, taken down
by Rybnikov; in general it is a variant of the narrative about the
Tiberian sea. Here the Lord and Satan strike with hammers
upon a rock and create for themselves armies, which instantly
fall to fighting. Such also is the tale from the far north, recorded by Barsov, where Sabaoth gives Satan a hammer and commands him to strike upon a stone mountain. As long as Satan
kept striking with his right hand, there flew forth angels that
bowed before God; but when he became tired, he struck with his
left hand, and there flew forth a black devil that bowed before
Satan. Then Satan hammered out for himself a whole army.

But similar tales are especially widespread among the non-
Slavic peoples in northeastern European Russia: the Cheremiss,
the Votyaks, the Mordvins. Among all these peoples the good
god and the devil strike out angels for themselves from the flint,
as sparks. This presents a unique expression of the old idea
concerning the creation of the angels out of fire; and the tales

of these peoples possess a greater originality than do the Great-Russian tales. In the Altaian tale (adduced by Veselovskij in Razyskanija XVIII-XXIV: 110), the devil (Erlik) creates the unclean spirits by hammering, as he does other beings. This idea is original, and at the same time it fits the region where from ancient times metals have been worked out. (Cf. also the creation through hammering in the other Turko-Altaian cosmogonic tale, which we have set forth above according to Radloff.)

On the basis of this comparative review of the tales about the creation of the angels and the devils, like that which has entered into the Bundle of Divine Books, we permit ourselves to entertain the idea that these tales were composed under the influence of Iranian[27] dualism, in Hither Asia; from there they have passed to the Turko-Finnic peoples of Russia, and later to the Russians themselves, among whom in the far north a similar tale had also been brought in a writing that was a compilation of cosmogony: the Bundle of Divine Books. However, we say in self-criticism, this assumption is far from verification.

In " The tale of how God created Adam," printed by Pypin from an Old Russian manuscript of the XII century, it says at the beginning: " . . . to create man in the land of Madiam, he took a handful of earth from the eight parts. . . . And the Lord God went to have eyes from the sun and he left Adam lying alone on the earth; there came then the Accursed Soton to Adam and smeared him with mud and slime. . . . And the Lord came to Adam and would place eyes in Adam, and he saw him a man smeared. And the Lord became wroth with the devil and he began to speak: Accursed devil, damned one, is not thine own perdition enough? Why with respect to this man hast thou created his perdition by smearing him? And damned shalt thou be — And the devil vanished like lightning from the earth from before the face of the Lord. And the Lord, to remove from him the mischief of Soton, therefore the Lord created the dog, and having mixed also a paste(?) with Adam's tears he cleaned him like a mirror from all filth, and he set the dog and bade him watch over Adam, and the Lord went alone to upper Jerusalem for a spirit for Adam. And Soton came a second time and would pour upon Adam evil filth, and he saw the dog lying by Adam's knees, and Soton was much affrighted. The dog began to bark evilly at the devil, so the accursed Soton having taken a stick, he pierced the man Adam everywhere and made in him seventy illnesses.

And there came Jesus from the upper Jerusalem, and he saw
Adam pricked all over by the stick and he had pity on him and
he said to Soton: Damnéd devil, what hast thou done to this man,
why hast thou placed these illnesses within him? Then answered
the devil, the accursed Soton, Lord, he said, if there come to
this man some illness, as long as it shall last, to its end he shall
mention thee; if he be taken sick, whatever infirmity he suffer
within him, then ever he will call upon thee for help in all infirmities. And the Lord drove away the devil and the devil vanished,
driven away like the darkness by the light, and he changed all
the infirmities to within him" i.e., within the man's body (Pypin:
Ložnyja i otrečennyja knigi russkoj stariny: 12-13).

About this tale it must be observed that it is not met with
in any of the ancient apocryphas which speak of Adam's creation.
Aside from this, the whole is edited too wordily even for this
manuscript in which it occurs; therefore it looks as though it had
been inserted, and that by some nothern Great-Russian — to
judge by the spelling of the name Soton. It does not harmonize
with the Bogomil notions; for according to the Bogomils the body of man is created by Satan.[28] Moreover, even the tone of the
tale does not correspond with the serious role of Satan in the
Bogomil view. This tale is very widespread in Russia and Siberia. But in the Balkan peninsula it is recorded only in Bulgaria; and then only in a very brief form:

"The Lord first created the giants and the dwarfs, and then
he realized that people should be more flexible and sinewy; and,
so as to make them that way, he took and made them of mud and
put them in the shade to evaporate, and then in the sun to dry
out. At this time came the devil, with the purpose of spoiling
God's nice creation and to do mischief to God for his handiwork;
he took and poked holes in the man's body with his stick and so
pierced it through in some places. When the Lord came back,
and saw what shamefulness the devil had wrought upon the man's
body, he thought to conserve at least the form of his handiwork
and so he took and gathered up grass, which he stuffed into the
holes and the folds from the Devil's proddings, and then he
smeared the man with the mud, and healed him and he became
whole. And whenever man's body becomes sick, if there should
happen to be among the medicines used to heal it some weed of
the grasses with which the Lord stopped up and cleansed the
man's body, he would recover and become well. And this is

the source of the healing-power of herbs and weeds." (Sbornik za nar. umotvorenija, etc. II: 165).

It is obvious that this story contains nothing about the be-smirching of the man and about the dog.[29]

In the Ukraine, a similar tale is recorded in entirety only in the east, near Great-Russia, where it is very widespread, as we have said:

God molded man out of clay, and left him to dry. He placed the dog to guard him, while he himself went off somewhere. The dog watched and watched, he became cold, and fell asleep. The dog at that time was naked, without a fur. The devil passed by, saw the man, tore his chest open, hawked and bespittled him, and put him together as he was before. God came, breathed into man an immortal soul, and he hawked. And God said to the dog, "How is it that you have not watched him as you should?" "Well," said he, "I was cold, and I fell asleep. Give me fur and I will then watch him faithfully." Then God took and gave him a fur, while man remained forever with the wetnesses inside him. (Dragomanov: Malorussk. nar. pred. i razsk. :I. Recorded in the Kharkov uyezd). We note that here there is not a word about boring holes into the man's body, nor about illnesses.

In the more southwestern parts of the Ukraine such tales exist in much atrophied form.

In the Kiev government it is told that the first man was very beautiful, while the devil was wretched and a limper. Out of spite for man's beauty, the devil bespittled him. God put inside the man all the spittle that covered him. Since then man is al-ways spitting, but he cannot spit himself out. (Čubinskij, Trudy ekspeditsii I: 145). Here too the dog is absent. In other stories it occurs, though not in the role of a watch but in that of a mar-plot;[30] thus, in one it is said that God modeled man first out of a wheat lump and put him in the sun to dry — and the dog ate him up. Then God made man out of clay. In another tale, God made the man out of clay and the woman out of dough; he put them to dry and commanded Michael to guard them. Michael guarded and guarded, but then he began to yawn a bit, and the dog ran up and ate the woman. God then made another out of bone from Adam's rib (ibid.).

The last anecdote has served in the Ukraine as a point of departure for the quite humorous tale about the Polish boyars:

When the Lord made the various nations, he made the
Muscovites, the Frenchmen, the Tatars, the Chinese; he still
had to make the Poles, but there was not enough clay. He made
the Pole out of dough and arranged all of (the peoples) next to
each other, and went off by himself. The dog comes running;
he smells one — clay; another — clay; he smells the Pole —
bread. He seizes him and eats him up. God comes back; he
blows and blows — the Muscovite begins to walk; he breathes
and breathes — the Frenchman walks. All the peoples walk
off, but there is no Pole! Where is the Pole? The dog has eat-
en him up. The Lord goes after him and catches up with him
on the bridge. He hits him from the bridge — out jumps Pan
Mostowicki; he hurls him down on the ground — out jumps Pan
Zemnacki; he slaps him on the belly — Pan Brjuchowecki —
and now all of those there Pan's, look at 'em go look at 'em go!
(Dragomanov: Malorusskija nar. predanija i razskazy). In the
White-Russian variant of this tale God molded the Polish
šljaxtič's (boyars) out of cheese. (Etnografičeskoe Obozrěnie
XII-XIII: 252). The Lithuanians have a similar tale in the Vilna
government: God molded his man out of clay, and the devil made
his out of dough. The dog passed by and ate up the dough man
of the devil. The devil became angry, and he seized the dog by
the tail. From fright the dog defecated, and the devil's handiwork came out again. From it came the boyars; from God's
man, the common folk. (Etnografičeskoe Obozrenie VI: 139-
140).[31]

It is clear that in the Ukraine, as in Bulgaria, the tale of
the spoiling of man's body by the devil and of the dog's presence
at that time, has been dying out. If we take the other peoples
into comparison, we shall conclude that the Slavic south has not
been the home of similar tales.

The tales of the spoiling of Adam's body by the devil are
spread throughout Great-Russia, and in more complete form
than the Kharkov tale (see Veselovskij). Their slight difference
from the Kharkov tale is the detail that, in them the devil de-
files the man on the outside, and God turns him inside out, thus
putting all the filthiness inside.[32]

Quite similar tales to the Great-Russian we find in abun-
dance among the non-Slavic nations of northeastern European
Russia and northern Asia, even among such as do not have the
dualistic legend like the Russian; e.g., the Samoyeds. The tale

of how the devil spoiled man's body that was being guarded by the dog is found among the Cheremiss, the Votyaks, the Mordvins, the Samoyeds, the Altaian Turks, the Mongols, the Buryats, the Yakuts, the Kirghiz. (All of them have been extracted and collected by Veselovskij; the Kirghiz variant is printed in Etnografičeskoe Obozrěnie VIII: 250-252). Among all these peoples we find in the tale a new detail with respect to the Great-Russian variants, namely: the devil wins the dog over to his side, by promising him a pelt. This detail answers to the demiurgic role of the devil in the systems which resemble the Manichean, and it gives to these non-Slavic variants in Russia and northern Asia the character of a greater antiquity as over against the Great-Russian. In one of the Altaian variants the demiurgic role of the devil (Shulmus) in this episode is so elevated that he even breathes a spirit into the body of the man, which had been left by the other two creators. In another variant, Mai-dere creates seven male humans and beside them seven trees, and into the men he breathes spirits. But after seven years the trees had grown branches, but the people had not multiplied. Then Mai-dere peeled off a woman and then a snake; breathed into the latter and wound it around the figure of the woman, and put the dog to guard the woman. The devil (Erlik) tempted the dog by promising him a fur coat, and breathed a spirit into the woman through a fife with seven stops, playing on his whistle with seven tongues. The spirit of the woman was evil, and her mind always of seven kinds, with seven tongues of different notes, and her body stinks. Later Mai-dere created for one of the men a new woman, taking from her sides two bones apiece (Veselovskij: Razyskanija XVIII-XXIV: 108-109, from materials of Verbitskij and Landyšev"; variant in Etnografičeskoe Obozrěnie VIII: 250-252).

Such details cannot be derived at all from the Russian apocryphas and folk tales: they are older and fuller than the Russian.[33]

In general, on the question of the borrowing between Russians and aborigines in northeastern Russia and in Siberia, we shall remark that the Russian common people does not occupy itself with special propaganda of its religious views. But from the missionaries the aborigines receive canonical notions, and not apocryphal ones, mostly names only (Jesus, Mary, St. Nicholas, etc.) which they mix into their theologies. Meanwhile the aborigines themselves, as they gradually appropriate the Russian language and so change over into Great-Russians, must bring into the Great-Russian folklore a whole mass of their tales and beliefs. And such a process of Russianization has been going on from time immemorial, under the very eyes of history, from the IX century onward.

It is a striking thing that the Magyar tale of how the devil made the cold and deceived the guardian dog, bespittled the man and put diseases into him, is much nearer the tales of the Finno-Turkic peoples in Russia than to the Ukrainian.[34] This compels us to think that the Magyars have brought this tale out of Ugria near the Urals, and not that they have obtained it from their Slavic neighbors.

However, we must take note of a phenomenon which perhaps runs counter to our hypothesis concerning the movement of the tales reviewed; namely, the extraordinary closeness of a Lithuanian tale, recorded in the Vilna government, to the Altaian. In this Lithuanian tale it is said that God formed Adam, and the devil Eve. But the devil, when he discovered that with his quill he could not breathe a spirit into his creation, took the quill which God had left after he had breathed a spirit into Adam, and with it he began to breathe a spirit into his own glue-work, Eve. Since in the quill there still was a little of God's breath, Eve came to life; but the devil added his own to her spirit. (Etnografičeskoe Obozrěnie VI: 141). Can it be that the Lithuanians have taken the basis of this tale from the Tatars who were settled in considerable numbers by their princes in the Vilna government, and of whom Mohammedan remnants still live there to this day?

On the basis of this survey of the variants of the spoiling of Adam's body by the devil and of the dog, it is easier to assume that this tale has spread among the Slavs from the east, rather than the reverse — from the Slavs, moving to the eastern peoples. And, to judge by the oral tales, it must have been precisely in northern Great-Russia that it was added to the apocrypha, in comparatively recent times, without any admixture from the Old Bulgarian literature.

If our surmises about the apocryphal and legendary motifs just reviewed have any validity, we shall obtain a clue that is very interesting for understanding the Slavic apocryphas; namely, that they have not remained immobile in the various Slavic lands. These apocryphas, to be sure, must have passed even as far as northeastern Russia out of Asia Minor and Greece through Bulgaria; but in the course of time they underwent reworking and received new overlays, even when in the spirit of the ancient motifs. Thus, in Bulgaria itself, in the Discourse of the Three Prelates there is the addition about the devil as Samuel; while in Great Russia, out of the brief and ancient notes as to the number of the parts out of which Adam was created, there grew up a whole tale about his body; while out of the note about the former greatness and later fall of Satan there grew up whole stories about the diver-Satanail and the creation of God's angels out of the one half of the stone which Satanail extracted from the sea, while Satanail's angels came from the other half. The material for these stories both the Bulgarians and the Great-Russians must have taken from the oral tales which came to them from Asia, both Hither and Northern, where these tales represent a reworking of the ancient cosmogonic legendary motifs, particularly the Irano-Chaldean.

The wave of the Asiatic cosmogonic notions, which has moved in Europe's direction from the most ancient times of the Persian kingdom of the Achaemenids (if not earlier), would hardly be gathered in its entirety exclusively into Biblical frame, but also into the frame of the literature called apocryphal, among this being the Bogomil. This wave traveled also by an oral channel. Simultaneously, this does not exclude the possibility of there taking shape in separate places, and so among the Slavic peoples, a number of variants upon a common dualistic theme. It is the task of comparative research to unravel these written and oral tales into their component elements and to point out the genesis of each of them. In such investigation it is indispensable that the common ideational currents be indicated. But it is not allowable to forget the differences between the various stories; it is not allowable to reduce all things down to one common measure in a generally analogical way, whether they be Biblical, Iranian, or apocryphal or particularly Bogomil. Thereupon, in referring the several folk stories to such comparatively late beliefs and legends as the written ones of the Middle Ages (whether canonical or heretical), it is not allowable to forget the matter of the more ancient sources of the latter. Careful scrutiny may reveal that the similarity between various beliefs and legends, between the ethnic and the written, is explainable in that the former have been influenced immediately by precisely these older sources. Of course, in the case of many stories, we shall not be able to express ourselves definitively; but for the present it is enough to place the questions under a strict methodology that is both synthetic and analytic.

Notes

1. See Stade: Geschichte des Volkes Israel; Piepenbring: Théologie de l'ancien testament; Schenkel: Bibel-Lexikon (art. ENGEL, SATAN UND DÄMONEN, et al.); Herzog: Real-Encyclopädie der protest. Theologie (art. ENGEL, TEUFEL, et al.); Kohut: Über die jüdische Angelologie und Demonologie in ihrer Abhängigkeit vom Parsaismus; Spiegel: Avesta, et al.

2. That according to the ancient Hebrew beliefs Jehovah did not hesitate to instil through his angels ruinous ideas into the kings to destroy them, is seen also in the characteristic place in I Kings XXII: 19-23, where Jehovah, desiring to destroy King Ahab, asks his angels: "Who shall persuade Ahab, that he may go up and fall at Ramath-gilead?" One of the spirits stands forth and says, "I will persuade him." Wherewith? "I will go forth and I will be a lying spirit in the mouth of all his prophets." In the familiar tale of Saul's mental illness there troubles him "an evil spirit from the Lord." And in the Greek translation it stands, πνεῦμα πονηρὸν παρὰ τοῦ κυρίου I Sam. XVI: 14-16, 23.

3. For the Egyptian representations of Set and Apopis see Brugsch: Religion und Mythologie der alten Aegypter nach den Denkmälern, II B, 102 seq.; and Wiedemann: Die Religion der altern Aegypter 117 seq. Maspero tries to bring to the examination of the ancient Egyptian religion a truly historical-evolutionar method in his articles on La Mythologie égyptienne, in Revue historique des religions, XVIII and XX.

4. For collections of the data concerning Iranian dualism, see the translations of the Avesta by Spiegel, de Harlez, and Darmsteter and the explanatory notes on them; also Justi: Der Bundahisch; Spiegel: Eranische Alterthumskunde und die traditionelle Literatur der Persen; Darmsteter: Ormazd et Ahriman; Windischmann: Zoroastrische Studien. The definitive edition of the Avesta, especially of the Bundahish, is very late — it took place, in fact, in the time of the Sassanids. But according to the data furnished us by comparing the Iranian beliefs with the Aryan Vedic, and likewise according to information

among the classicists, we can assert that the basic teachings of
the Iranian dualism, namely, the belief in a dualistic world-
creation, in the temporary indulgence of Ahriman's power, in
sending the teacher-messiah Zoroaster and the elimination of
Ahriman's power, etc., existed among the Iranians before the
IV century B.C., and in its rudiments even earlier. Among
other things, in the Iranian books it is told that Ormuzd's servants often subdued various snakelike and dragonlike creations
of Ahriman and confined them underground.

5. In the name Asmodeus many (Graetz, Spiegel, Kohut,
et al.) see an Iranian name Esma-Deva or Dasya — one of the
spirits (daevas) of Ahriman: Aeshma. Isr. Levi attempts to
dispute this (Revue des études juives 1884, I: 64). For Aeshma
see de Harlez: Avesta, Index. However, our own opinion is
that the whole basis of the Book of Tobit is to be found in the
Indian legendary history of Vikramaditya (in both parts: "Twenty-
five tales of the horde" in the Mongolian edition, and "Thirty-
two tales of the throne"), and it is one of the parallels to the
tales of the grateful corpse, which occur also among the Bulgarians; beside the variants which we have had occasion to adduce
here, see Sborn. za nar. umotv. VIII: iii: 178-180, where in
a note on a Prilep variant there are cited also a few foreign
variants.

6. Translation of the American Revised Version adapted
to fit Dragomanov's quotation. EWC

7. In the Bible these angels are named for the first time
in the Book of Daniel (VIII: 16, IX: 21, X: 13, 21, XII: 1), which
the new exegesis places in the mid-II century B.C. in the epoch
of the struggle of the Maccabees with the Syrian kingdom.
(Cornill: Einleitung in das alte Testament, 1891, 256-260).

8. So in the Greek; although not in the standard English
translations. EWC

9. Cf. in the Zend Avesta how Ahriman tempts Ormuzd:
Vendidad III, Fargard VI: 20-26 (trans. de Harlez, 192-193;
trans. Spiegel I: 142-143). It is interesting to compare these
brief tales from the Zend Avesta with the more extended Indian
tales of the temptation of Buddha, which the most recent European amateurs of Buddhism consider the source of the Christian
(Rudolf Seydel: Das Evangelium von Jesu in seinen Verhältnissen
zur Buddhasage und Buddhalehre, 156-165). It seems to us that
the Iranian tale is more at home in the dualistic system of the
Avesta than in the history of Buddha, and could have served as
the source both of the Buddhistic and of the western stories.

10. Dragomanov translates into Bulgarian from the translations under the editorship of Kautzsch: <u>Die heilige Schrift des alten Testaments</u>, and that of Reuss: <u>La Bible, Les Prophètes II</u>: 190. I have chosen to transcribe correspondingly from the American Revised Version. EWC

11. Langlois: <u>Rig-Veda</u>, 91 (Sec. I, sect. 6, h. 3, v. 10); A. Maury: <u>Croyances et légendes de l'antiquité</u>, 64.

12. Darmsteter: <u>Ormazd et Ahriman</u>, 332.

13. I. A. Eisenmenger: <u>Entdecktes Judenthum</u>, 1711, II B. 370-371, 409-410.

14. Eisenmenger, op.cit. 371, 412-415.

15. Schenkel: <u>Bibel-Lexikon</u>, ENGEL; Eisenmenger, op. cit. 371.

16. Eisenmenger, op. cit. 412.

17. Eisenmenger, op.cit. 411; Weil: <u>Biblische Legenden der Muselmänner</u>, 16; Porfirjev'': <u>Skazanija o vetxozavětnyx'' licax'' i sobytijax''</u>, izslědovanie 35-66.

18. Koran II: 28-32; VIII: 11. Weil, op.cit. 12-16. The notion that the devil fell because he was unwilling to submit to Adam comes out in the Slavic apocrypha "Prěpirnja Isusə Xristovə sə djavola", printed in Tixonravov'': <u>Pamjatn. otreč. liter</u>. II: 282-288. The influence of this apocrypha can be discerned in the beginning of the Ukrainian tale printed in <u>Etnograf. Obozrěnie</u>, vv. XIII-XIV, where Satan (the Wise Danil) does not consent to bow down to the Son of God, before whom God had commanded the whole panoply of heaven to pass in review. The Great-Russian influence is discernible in these tales.

19. Eisenmenger, op.cit. II: 432-433, 463, 467-488. The notion of Ahriman's repentance occurs in the later Iranian books.

20. See also the "Šestodnev" or the Creation of the World ("The Six Days" — EWC) by the Severian who died in 415 A.D.; an essay which has been attributed to John Chrysostomus; I: 5. Consult Migne: "Patrologiae cursus completus, series graeca," LVI: 435. Its Slavonic translation is found further in the manuscripts of the Kazan library. For the doctrines of Marcion, Valentinus, and the Manicheans, see also the "Šestodnev" of Vasil the Great (Migne, op.cit. XXIX, hom. II in Hexameron I: 4, XXX: 885; and the "Šestodnev" of John the Exarch of Bulgaria (<u>Opisanie rukopisej Kazanskoj biblioteki</u>, 114).

21. Lactantii Institutiones II: 9.

22. Various passages in the doctrines of the Church Fathers
of the III and IV centuries are cited in Roskoff: Geschichte des
Teufels, 1869, I: 220-223, 267-268. See also the interesting
excerpts from the homilies of George the Great in the article
about Michael and the angels among the Bolandists — Acta
Sanctorum, Septembris, die xxix, tom. VIII: 8-10. On the
matter of how in time the account in the Book of Enoch concerning Michael's war with those angels who had united with the
daughters of men became attenuated among the Church Fathers,
and of how this same account came to be considered heretical,
consult Roskoff op.cit. I: 267-268. Interesting data on the
Ancient Egyptian and Syro-Phoenician elements in the Christian
and Moslem legends of St. George's (Moslem: Khidr, identified
with St. Elias, and the latter with Helios) and St. Michael's combat with the dragon are presented in the memoir of Clermont-
Ganneau, in connection with the relief of the Egyptian Horus with
a bird's face, garbed as a Roman officer, mounted on a horse,
and defeating Set-Typhon in the shape of a crocodile: Revue
archéologique 1876, Septembre-Décembre: Horus et Saint-George
d'après un bas-relief inédit du Louvre.

23. Set rules the north and sits upon Ursus Major. See
Brugsch, loc. cit. In the Talmud accounts the devils occupy
the northern region: Eisenmenger, op.cit. 438, 439.

24. Cf. above, Miška and Griška and Satan in the Ukrainian tale.

25. Vasakomə. Perhaps a dialectic variant of vsjakomə:
"everything"(?). EWC

26. So also in the Serbo-Bulgarian manuscript in the Vienna
University library (Sign. I: 120) described by Polivka in
Etnografičeskoe Obozrěnie VIII: 252-253: "(Question:) And how
did God create the devil? (Answer:) When the Lord looked and
beheld his shadow in the water, he said: Come forth, brother,
and be with me. There came forth a man and he called his
name Anatail. When the Lord planted Paradise, then as he
commanded him to plant Atail (sic — EWC) stole of all the
fruits and he scattered (them) in the midst of Paradise unbe-
known to the Lord. The Lord said: Thou didst steal from me,
let it be for thy banishment; depart, Satanail. And he said,
Lord, bless what we have planted. The Lord said; It is
blessed, I rule in the midst, thou shalt have no rule. Satanail departed to see the tree which he had planted of what
he had stolen, and he saw the tree. Then Satanail became
black. (The Lord) expelled his tree from Paradise, then

(he) called him devil." Here the devil is called also Samuel.

27. Dragomanov has "Ukrainian"; which undoubtedly is a misprint. EWC.

28. In an Ukrainian tale in Čubinskij (Trudy ekspedicii I: 145), Satan gives also a soul to the man. Here it is said further that Satan, after making the man, stood him upright. Obviously both tales are altered and atrophied from the Bogomil belief transmitted by Zigabenus.

29. Among the Bulgarians there is a particular tale about the creation of the dog, according to which God created him from the intestines of Abel's corpse, to guard the sheep after Abel's death (Šapkarev: Sbornik za narodni starini III: 6-7).

30. "Вращ" — "vračə": sorcerer. Sic. this is senseless. I have emended to "Врагъ": "vragə": antagonist. Hence, technically, "marplot." EWC

31. In Bulgaria there is an (aristocratic) tale quite different in content and character about the derivation of the various classes. They are derived from the children of Eve whom she failed to wash and clothe for a visit to God (Sbornik za nar. umotv. II: 192-193). It is interesting that in Bielorussia they tell that Eve's hidden children gave rise to the wood-spirits (Romanov": Bělorusskij Sbornik" IV: 157). There is a chauvinistic Hungarian tale about the creation of the various nations: Slovak, proletariat, German (Wlisłocki: Volksglaube und religiöser Brauch der Magyaren, 95). The rather aristocratic Imeretian tale of the derivation of the classes is also interesting: Sbornik" mater. dlja opisanija Kavkaza IX: 174-175.

32. In Bielorussia, where there are recorded several variants of the tale of Satan's diving for earth, there is no record of a tale about how the devils were struck down, nor of one about how Adam's body was defiled.

33. We recall the sacred significance of the dog in ancient Iran (Avesta, transl. de Harlez, 137 etc., Vendidad, Farg. XIII); a concept which Islam attacked when later it penetrated Central Asia. Still later, the snake and the dog take the shape of Mitresums in the scene of the beginning of creation. It is not irrelevant to remark that there are Talmudic tales in which God created for Adam different wives out of different materials. First he created the woman Lilith out of earth; but she considering herself Adam's equal refused to lie under him; she flew to heaven and became a demonic being. Then God created Eve

from Adam's rib (Eisenmenger, op.cit. 417-419). Perhaps further research will disclose the connection between these tales and some of those just given, or with the Ukrainian tale of the creation of two wives for Adam (see Ch. V).

34. H. v. Wlisłocki: Volksglaube und religiöser Brauch der Magyaren, 94. On p. 93 there is also another variant that has arisen out of an alteration of the first: the dog seized Adam's rib which God had prepared for creating Eve, so God made Eve out of the dog's tail. That is why "it is all one and the same thing — to entrust a secret to a woman's tongue or to hang yourself with a dog's tail." According to the Bulgarian tale published in Sbornik za nar. umotvor. IX: 155, woman was created from the devil's tail. God sent an angel to take a rib from Adam's body to make Eve from it; but before the angel could present himself before God, who had lain down to sleep, the devil deceived the angel and took the rib away from him; and as the angel was unable to get it back again, he merely pulled off the devil's tail and returned to God to tell him what had happened and to complain about the devil. God, still drowsy, and thinking that the angel was holding Adam's rib as ordered, said: "Let what is in your hands become what I told you." Immediately the devil's tail in the hands of the angel turned into a woman. In the notion that the dog ate up the material for the creation of Eve, the second Magyar tale resembles an Ukrainian variant. In its further elaboration of this idea, in its despising of women, the Magyar variant recalls the spirit of the Central Asiatic tale according to which the devil breathed a soul into the woman's body. However, the latter case may be no more than a coincidence.

ADDENDA

Addendum to Ch. III. — On beliefs of the Yezids.

Sheik-Adi and Melek-Taus. — Periods of cosmogony. —
Figures on the temple walls: the world-tree with cross, doves,
snake with tree. — The snake saves Noah. — Traces of Mithraism. — The quaking aspen.

After the first half of this study had been printed, there
appeared J. Menant's little book, Les Yézids. Here we find
some new data on the beliefs of this people which may be pro-
fitably noted here. The Englishman Badger (Nestorians and
Their Rituals) questioned one of the spiritual leaders of the Yezids about the persons they revered; he received the answer
that Sheik-Adi has no father, but proceeds from out of the light
and will not die; that he is the creator of the good while the creator of evil is Melek-Taus; at present the latter is fallen, but
after a time he will again be with the good god, who will give
him another place. As in the Bundahish etc., the Yezids believe
in cosmogonic periods (Menant, op.cit. 90-92, 87). On the walls
of the chief Yezid temple there are various sculptured figures
the meaning of which the Yezids no longer understand or else
they do not wish to explain to outsiders. One of these figures
arrests our attention: on the outside of the temple, quite at the
top and directly above the door, are the figures of two doves
next to a figure of a (cosmic) tree; on the right there are two
doves, one above the other; farther below, two dogs, again beside such a tree that is signalized by a cross; still farther down,
on the same side and to the right, a snake and a tree; beside
the snake a comb — as it were, the symbol of woman, a thing
which elsewhere is encountered also in conjunction with a crook,
the symbol of a man.
On the inside it is interesting to see to the left of the door
the dual figure of the sacred tree with garlands above it, shaped

like snakes, and farther down another figure of the same sort
though more schematized.*

The figure of the snake belongs to the oldest parts of the
temple. The Yezids supply no explanation for this figure, but
they relate that when Noah was floating in the ark, the ark was
punctured on the peak of Mt. Sinjar; and it would have sunk had
not Noah persuaded the snake to lie along the place where the
plank was shattered. It is noteworthy that also in the Magyar
legend of the deluge — interesting further for its misogyny
(H. v. Wlisłocki: Volksglaube und religiöser Brauch der Magyaren, 103) — the snake saves the ark in the same way after
being bitten by the devil transformed into a mouse. In the same
way, in the Ukrainian tales, Noah's ark was saved by the adder
(a non-venomous snake); wherefore God removed its venom
(Ivanov'': Iz'' oblasti malorusskix'' narodnyx'' legend''; Etnograf.
Obozr. 1893, 2, pp. 71-72). We shall refrain from expressing
an opinion as to any possible connection between these depictions
and the Indian variants of the deluge tale in which the snake was
provender for Manu's boat.

The sun-worship of the Yezids obviously recalls Irano-
Chaldean Mithraism, which had achieved such wide occurrence
in Europe during Roman times as the cult of the unconquered
sun — Mithra. And in the Sofia museum there are two reliefs
which depict with very interesting details Mithra slaying the
bull to create the world. In that here it is the Sun-god who slays
the bull, and not Ahriman — who in the Bundahish destroys the
primal bull — this indicates the transformation the ancient Iranian
beliefs suffered as they migrated westward through Mesopotamia.
The Yezids, who worship the rising sun even to this day, also
deify the bull like the Mithraists; they term it the mediator between god and man, as was Mithra the Sun among the Iranians
(Menant, op. cit. 117-118).**

Of the Yezid beliefs that have interest for comparisons
with the Slavic we shall note the belief concerning the quaking

---

*Dragomanov reproduces figures borrowed by Menant from
Badger, op. cit. I: 107. EWC

**It is interesting to compare with the usual relief of the
Mithraists the Assyrian figure in which the bull stands before
the world-tree. See Lenormant: Histoire ancienne de l'Orient,
I: 36.

asp (<u>Populus</u> tremulus). The Yezids hold this tree sacred,
saying that Jesus' cross was made of it (Menant, p. 86). In the
Ukrainian beliefs the quaking asp appears now as a sacred tree
now as accursed. Once it is related that it was specially created
by God, and that is why an aspen stake is driven into the grave
or into the bodies of witches and vampires; again it is considered
accursed precisely for these same customs. And to this they
add that when Joseph and Mary were fleeing from Herod into
Egypt they hid under a quaking asp; and all the trees became
silent except the quaking asp, which kept rustling its leaves.
They tell moreover that it was on the quaking asp that Judas
hanged himself. The latter belief they sometimes transfer to
the elder, saying further that on this tree St. Barbara was hanged.
Elsewhere they say that it was from the osier that the nails were
made for Christ's crucifixion (Čubinskij, <u>Trudy</u> I: 76-77).

All these beliefs echo the eastern ones like the Yezid, and
they have become distorted and confused in Europe. There is
no reason for us to tarry further over them; we shall limit ourselves merely to indicating that somewhere there is a connection
between these beliefs and the eastern, on the basis of the Yezid
beliefs. Thus, near Cairo they showed the European traveler
Tevenot the sycamore (?) in which the Mother of God hid with
Christ (Brunet: <u>Les Evangiles apocryphes</u>, 102-103; cf. how
Rama's mother sat on a tree: <u>Journal Asiatique</u> 1847, p. 487).
For elucidating the tree involved in the deaths of Jesus, Judas,
et al., it is interesting to adduce an extract from the rare Jewish
essay against the Christians by Toldos Jeschu, published in
Latin translation by Wagenseilius: "Tela ignea Satanae, hoc est
arcani et horribiles Judaeorum adversus Christum Deum et
Christianam Religionem libri Anekdotoi (Altdorfi Noricorum.
1681)." In this essay (p. 18), among other things it is told that
when they were stoning Jesus and ordering that he be crucified,
there was no tree that could hold him (in this essay, Jesus is
portrayed as a powerful magician). Jesus' disciples began to
boast of this. Whereupon Judas (who here is portrayed as a
yet more powerful magician) contrived it so that the weight of
Jesus' body was supported by one stalk of cabbage that grew in
his garden ("brassicae caulis ingens").

It is to just such a source that we must refer also the Serbian tradition of the <u>smrdljanka</u>, which formerly bore olives

but later was cursed by God after some king had hanged a righteous man on it (V. Karadjić: Život i običaji srp. nar., p. 231).

In the Bulgarian Christmas carols the quaking asp is accursed
for motives other than those in the Ukrainian beliefs. Thus e.g.,
John Baptist cursed it because it did not stand still when the
"young God" was being baptized (Sborn. za nar. umotv. I: iii,
5-6; cf. also the anecdote in Per. Spis. XXV, 198); St. John
cursed it because it did not become quiet when a star sang
above his banquet (Iliev: Sbornik za nar. umotv. obič. etc.,
148-149); St. Peter cursed it for a similar reason (ibid., 84.
For a similar Serbian song, see Karadjić, loc. cit., 230-231.

For various accursed trees see also Veselovskij: Razyskanija VII: 245.

Addendum to Chs. I and V.

A new variant to the cosmogonic Christmas carol.

This essay had been completely set up in type when we received this year's September issue of the Galician-Ukrainian
journal Pravda, published in Galicia, which in the article
Narodni Zvyčai, obrjady ta pisni v seli Krexovi, Žovkivskago
povitu contains a new variant of the cosmogonic Christmas carol
already adduced in Ch. I and discussed in Ch. V. This variant
is much closer to Vagilevič's variant which we copied, than that
cited above from Kievska Starina (1889: #1). For this reason
it is important, since it permits us to verify the authenticity of
that recorded by Vagilevič. As Pravda has such a limited cir-
culation, we shall copy this variant:

> Oh what was there from the world's beginning,
>> Rejoice!
>> Rejoice, earth-dweller, unto us the Son of God is born!*
> Nothing there was but a watery sea,
> On this water a little tree,
> 5 On this tree two shoots,
> On these shoots two angels sit,
> And as they sit, they take counsel with God,
> What to do about creating the world:

*This refrain to be repeated after every verse.

"Let us dive into the black sea,
10 Let us fetch black earth,
Let us divide it into four parts:
From the first part a lovely sun,
From the other part a clear moon,
From the third part bright little stars,
15 From the fourth part sprigs of thatch."
    Spoke the sun: "Whither shall I go?
Oh I will go throughout the week from early morn,
I will light up mountains and valleys."
    Spoke the moon, "Whither shall I go?
20 Oh I will go in May below the (?) sky,
I will light up mountains and valleys."
    Spoke the little stars, "Whither shall we go?
Oh we will go with the dawn,
We will light up mountains and valleys."
25   Spoke the thatch, "Whither shall I go?
Oh I will go in May beneath the (?) sky,
I will raise the wheat-grain,
The wheat-grain and every corn of Spring."

From verse 15 on to the first motif of the Christmas carols
there has been attached another which occurs also in special
songs. But the first 14 verses show clear resemblance to the
Christmas carol of Vagilevič. Only a few of their traits are
new: the angels are represented as birds, and it is earth, not
golden or blue stone, that is extracted from the sea.

Addendum to Chs. II and V.

The figure of the world-tree and the cosmogonic parapher-
nalia connected with it in the Mesopotamian and Mediterranean
monuments.

To make clearer our account of the remnants of Irano-
Chaldean representations in the Mesopotamian, Trans-
Caucasian, and other traditions, and likewise our juxtaposition
of these representations in the Ukrainian Christmas carol of
the three doves on the plane-tree, and the notes on the world-
tree, the snake, and the billy-goat, we think it appropriate
to adduce a series of illustrations, most of them taken from

Assyro-Babylonian reliefs, cylinders, and impresses of myth-
ological subjects.*

     In #1 we see a number of gods before the tree of life.
Among them, on the left, stands the fish-shaped god Ea the
Creator (Dagon of the Palestinians). This picture is matched
by the representations in the Bundahish, Ch. XXVII, according
to which there stands in the midst of the sea a tree which har-
bors the seeds of life (of both plant growth and primeval god)
and which "a divine bird (Camrus) shakes every year; whereupon the seed becomes mixed with water, and (the star) Tistria
brings water. By this tree there grows the white, eternal haoma
above the stream Ardvisura." Haoma, a plant from which the
Iranians prepared their sacred drink, may be placed beside the
tree of the knowledge of good and evil, which also in the Bible
is distinct from the tree of life, even if not with perfect clarity.

     In ##2-8 we see developing the zoomorphic symbolization of
the gods, who are grouped about the tree of life, while the human shapes are constantly being transformed into birds.

     In ##5-6, a god in human shape, though winged, stands in
the middle between two gods whose shape is almost completely
avian, as though he were an intermediary between them — they
are quarreling — like Sheik Sinn in the Yezid tale. In #5 this
scene occurs beside the tree of life.

     #10 is a drawing of the sculptured figure of the Yezid sym-
bol (sinjak) of Melek-Taus in the form of a dove.

     #11 obviously represents the fight around the tree of life.
It seems that the billy-goat depicted on the right is attacking the
tree; while on the left one of the figures defending the tree has
a dog's body. The moon is on the side of the defenders.

     #12 represents a billy-goat and a doglike god by the tree of
life, above which is suspended the symbol of the supreme deity.
These two figures seem to us important for explaining why the
billy-goat has a demonic significance, a thing so widespread
in the demonology and folk beliefs of mediaeval Europe. They
are significant as parallels to the sacred status of the dog in
Iranian beliefs, and also to his role as guardian placed by the
Creator over the images of the first people in the Central Asiatic
and Russian cosmogonic tales.

---

     *Dragomanov's descriptions here should be understandable
even without the illustrations themselves. EWC

#13 represents a couple, divine or human, before the tree of life; further, a snake placed behind the woman. Lenormant (Histoire ancienne de l'Orient I: 35) sees in this an immediate illustration of what appears in the biblical tales of the sin-and-fall of the first people; but we shall permit ourselves the belief that it is illustrative of the yet more ancient Babylonian tale still unknown to us — in the Bible, the snake converses with Eve only.

#14 depicts a Phoenician vase figuring the tree of life and the snake.

In #15 the snake is curled about the cosmic egg by the tree of life or the world-tree on which the world will be placed. The depiction comes from one side of a medal struck in Thurii in honor of the Emperor Heliogabalus (218-222). The other side has a portrait of the emperor. Depictions of the cosmic egg occur among many peoples; among civilized nations they are developed most fully among the Indians. According to Greek Orphic tales Aphrodite emerged from an egg in the river Euphrates; there must be a Chaldean tradition at the base of this (Layard: Nineveh and Its Remains I: 457). According to Plutarch ("De Iside", 47) the Persians said that "Ormuzd, after creating 24 gods, put them into an egg; the demons of Ahriman (the snake), also 24, broke into the egg, and thus did evil commingle with good." The medal from Thurii belongs to the time when various ancient peoples were mingling their religious ideas and composing that often inconsistent fabric of which traces have remained among the traditions of peoples down to this day, particularly among such as the Yezid. It is interesting to compare the illustrations of the snake and the egg that we have adduced, with those given by Matter in his Histoire critique du gnosticisme; e.g. his Pl. X: 3 shows a medallion with a snake on one side and about it a superscription CABAΩ and IAΩ (Hebr. Yahweh, Bab. Ea): Pl. XI is an inscription, attributed to the sect of the Carpocratians, for desegregating* of possessions and of women, in Greek and Phoenician, with an address to Zoroaster (Zerades) and Pythagoras, the figure of a snake holding its tail in its mouth and so forming a circle, as in the Indian depictions (symbol of eternity); and in the center the cosmic egg. With such commingling of the symbols and traditions of a variety of peoples,

---

* "општуванье." EWC

the biblical snake began to take on various interpretations. For instance, the sect which earned the special name of snake-worshippers (Ophites) made of the snake which tempted Eve in the Bible and whose image Moses set up for the Hebrews to worship, the emancipator of Adam and Eve from the jealous demiurge of the Old Testament (Ialdabaoth); it became the harborer* of the divine Supreme Wisdom (Sophia), of the mother of that very demiurge who was born along with the Primal Jesus Christ (who is also the First Man — Adam Kadmon) from the primeval bosom (the Abyss — βύθos, and the Thought — Ἔννοια). See Matter, op.cit. II: 148 seq.; Baur: Geschichte der christlichen Kirche I: 192-195, 227.

Such comminglings and arbitrary interpretations of various details in the traditions from a variety of ancient peoples account for the fact that present-day folk traditions, representing as they do the débris and the remote echoes of those comminglings, are so full of contradictions; so for instance in the Bulgarian traditions there appears as creator and greater power at one time the personage termed god, at another time the one termed devil; and so forth.

#16 and #17 reproduce the exterior and the interior walls of the Yezid temple near Rabban Khormuzd in Kurdistan.

#18 reproduces a relief on the door of an Athenian church of the XI century. In the center is a figure, something halfway between the cross and the schematic depiction of the world-tree of the Assyrian drawing (#8); on each side is a peacock (Didron, op.cit. 373). To the Yezids, this is the symbol of Melek Taus. According to Arabian Moslem tales, the peacock drove the snake out of paradise so as to introduce there the devil Iblis (Weil: Biblische Legenden der Muselmänner, 20-23). Magyar representations have it that the peacock is a bird of the devil (H. v. Wlisłocki: Volksglaube und religiöser Brauch der Magyaren, 111); according to the Ukrainian, peacocks are devils reborn (Čubinskij: Trudy I: 58).

---

* преемница. EWC

DO NOT REMOVE

SLIP FROM POCKET

DEMCO

RUSSIAN AND EAST EUROPEAN SERIES

Russian and East European Institute
Indiana University

Thomas A. Sebeok, *Editor;* Robert F. Byrnes, William B.
Edgerton, Norman J. G. Pounds, Nicolas Spulber, and
Robert C. Tucker, *Associate Editors*

VOLUMES IN PRINT

Volumes in Preparation

Lilien's *English-Polish Dictionary* is also distributed in connection with the Series. Fascicles 1-19 are available at $1.50 each.

See the notice on the verso of the title page for information
on ordering volumes in the RUSSIAN AND EAST EUROPEAN SERIES